Cham-gria

Nothing says summer like sangria, or sangaree, as it's sometimes known in parts of the South. Spanish in origin, the wine concoction seeped into the country through Florida and Texas. This version uses a bit of the bubbly in the blend.

MAKES ABOUT 1 GALLON, ENOUGH TO SERVE 12 GENEROUSLY

3 oranges, sliced and halved

3 limes, sliced and halved

2 lemons, sliced and halved

1 cup sugar

1½-liter bottle fruity red wine

1 cup apricot brandy

½ cup triple sec or other orange-flavored liqueur

Juice of 2 limes

750-milliliter bottle inexpensive champagne or sparkling wine

1. Place the fruit in a pitcher or large bowl. Cover the fruit with the sugar and let the mixture sit at room temperature for about 1 hour.

2. Pour the wine, brandy, triple sec, and lime juice over the fruit and stir to dissolve the sugar. Chill the mixture for at least 30 minutes and up to several hours.

3. Just before serving, mix in the champagne and add enough ice cubes to make the drink really frosty. Serve the sangria over more ice, adding a few fruit slices to each serving. *Salud.*

Mango-Lime Spritzer

A refreshingly light cooler, this is good as a nonalcoholic beverage, too. Just replace the wine with more club soda or carbonated mineral water. SERVES 2

1 large ripe mango, peeled, pitted, and cut in chunks

Juice of 1 lime

1 cup dry white wine

½ cup club soda or carbonated mineral water

Lime slices, for garnish

Combine the mango and lime juice in a blender and puree. Add the wine and club soda and blend thoroughly. Pour the mixture through a strainer into two tall glasses. Add ice, garnish with the limes, and serve.

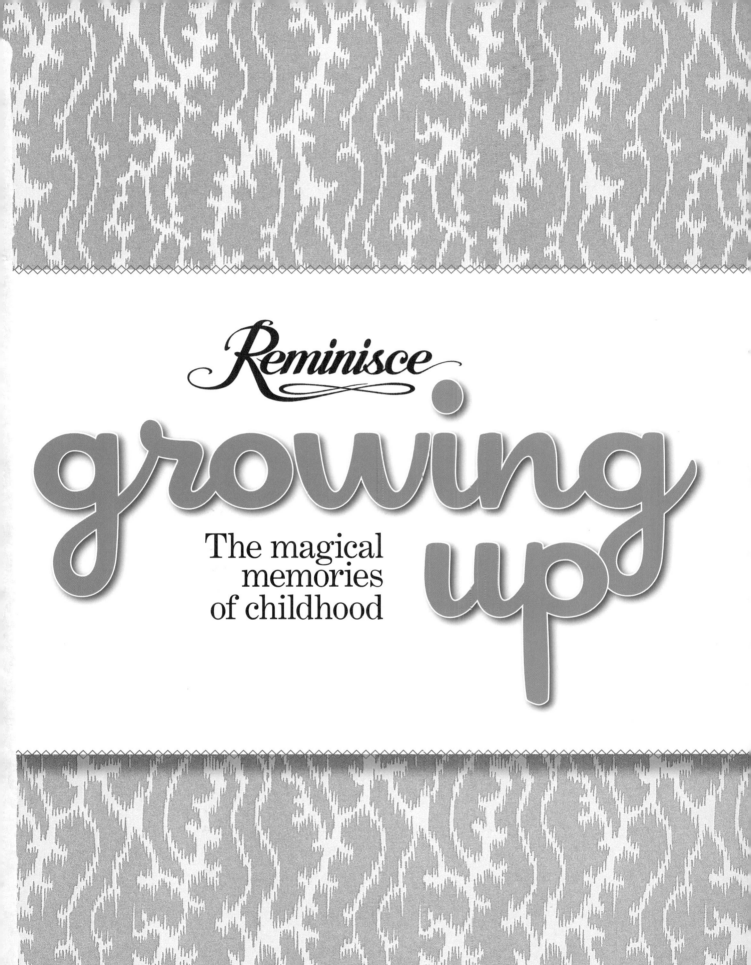

Reminisce

growing up

The magical memories of childhood

table of contents

page 6

page 30

page 56

page 80

page 100

page 124

page 146

page 164

page 184

REMINISCE: GROWING UP

Catherine Cassidy **Vice President, Editor in Chief**
Heidi Reuter Lloyd **Vice President, Executive Editor/Books**
Mark Hagen **Senior Editor/Books**
Julie Schnittka **Project Editor**
Angie Packer **Project Art Director**
Ellie Martin Cliffe **Associate Editor**
Sara Lancaster, Krista Lanphier, Michelle Rozumalski **Contributing Editors**
Heather Lamb **Executive Editor, Home & Garden**
Sharon K. Nelson **Creative Director, Home & Garden**
Julie Wagner **Content Production Manager**
Dena Ahlers **Production Coordinator**
Emma Acevedo **Design Layout Artist**
Deb Warlaumont Mulvey **Copy Chief**
Joanne Weintraub **Copy Editor**
Trudi Bellin **Photo Coordinator**
Mary Ann Koebernik **Assistant Photo Coordinator**
Barb Czysz **Administrative Assistant**

Bettina Miller **Editor/*Reminisce***
Cheryl A. Michalek **Art Director/*Reminisce***
John Burlingham **Senior Editor/*Reminisce***
Blanche Comiskey, Melody Trick **Editorial Assistants/*Reminisce***

Lisa Karpinski **North American Chief Marketing Officer**
Dan Fink **Vice President/Book Marketing**
Jim Palmen **Creative Director/Creative Marketing**

THE READER'S DIGEST ASSOCIATION, INC.
Mary G. Berner President and Chief Executive Officer
Suzanne M. Grimes President, North American Affinities

REMINISCE BOOKS
©2011 Reiman Media Group, LLC
5400 S. 60th St., Greendale WI 53129-1404

International Standard Book Number (10): 0-89821-850-0
International Standard Book Number (13): 978-0-89821-850-3

Library of Congress Control Number: 20093454

All rights reserved. Printed in U.S.A.
Cover image: SuperStock
For additional copies of this book or information on other books, write:
Reminisce Customer Service
P.O. Box 5294
Harlan IA 51593-0794
Call toll-free: 800-344-6913
e-mail: *rpsubscustomercare@custhelp.com*
Visit our website at *reminisce.com*

Kid years have a whole different pace
than adult years. For one thing, they seemed to last a lot longer. For adults, time flies. For kids, time is high-flyin'!

After months of school, for example, summer stretched into endless days of running around barefoot with friends, swimming, skipping rope, hopping on your bike and catching fireflies, while the adults sat on the front porch, chatting with neighbors.

We spent family times with Mom and Dad, grandparents, sisters and brothers and relatives, reunions and picnics and churning homemade ice cream.

Growing up wasn't always easy, of course. We had schoolwork and chores and were told what to do by grown-ups—but real adult responsibilities were still a long way off.

Thinking about growing up just makes you smile, and when you get older, you tend to appreciate it even more.

Remember when you couldn't wait for birthdays? Wow, that sure changes as an adult—but I can still recapture the magic if I think back on kid parties with cake and candles and ring-around-the-rosy. This is the power of fond memories, and that's why we put this special *Reminisce* book together, filled with precious photos and true stories recalling those wondrous years.

We've also added journal pages where you can write down your own fond childhood memories, creating a unique keepsake.

The pictures on this page are mine from childhood. One look sends me back in time—to the comfort of my mother's arms, the old swing set and hammock, my cute kitty Mitzi.

What a precious gift it is to look back on the carefree times. Happy reminiscing to you—and to the little kid who still lives in all of us.

Best to you all,

Bettina

Bettina Miller
Editor, *Reminisce* magazine

CLASSICSTOCK.COM

CHAPTER ONE

Precious Pets

From canines and cats to parakeets and ponies, pets are usually among the first friends kids make. You'd be hard-pressed to find someone more loyal to stand by you in times of trouble or more trustworthy with your deepest secrets. Not only did these critters offer unconditional love—they were the best playmates you could ask for!

Rex (shown in the photo below right) was a constant companion when Ila Russell and her older sister Ilene were growing up in the 1930s.

"He enjoyed the attention, but at times I'm sure he felt reluctant to be our playmate," admits Ila. "I'm not sure whose idea it was to play dress-up when this photo was taken at our uncle's farm near Forestville, Michigan, but we must have had help getting poor old Rex into that dress and hat. Although he may have suffered a bit, he certainly seems happy enough to take part in the picture-taking session!"

Yes, our treasured pets were always willing to put up with our childhood antics. Read on for more stories of how they warmed our hearts, became part of the family—and even caused an occasional commotion!

tarzan of new jersey

By Emil Knab, Cumming, Georgia

This is the story of a German shepherd that was a member of our family in Irvington, New Jersey, from 1932 until 1948. Tarzan came to us when he was about 8 weeks old and seemed highly intelligent—almost as if he understood everything we were saying.

He clearly recognized words like car, ice cream, store, money and go. Upon hearing them, he'd run to the door and stand there waiting for us.

Of course, there were times when we couldn't take him along. On those occasions, Mother would tell us in German, "Close the dog in the kitchen." (Luckily, Tarzan never learned German.)

Another sound he recognized was the jingling of coins. To him that meant we were going to the store, where we might buy him an ice cream Dixie Cup.

If we did, he'd take it outside, lie down with the cup between his paws and rotate it until he found the tab on the cover. Then he'd deftly remove the cover with his teeth and lap the ice cream out, leaving barely a tooth mark on the paper.

One day, my brothers, Jack and Carl, and I decided to find out how much Tarzan really understood. We jingled some change, and Tarzan immediately jumped up and ran to the door.

We showed him a nickel (the price of a Dixie Cup) and told him to take it to the store. He took the money in his mouth, ran down the stairs and out the door.

When we got to the store, he was waiting outside. We didn't know if he'd lost (or even swallowed) the nickel, but I asked him to drop the nickel if he wanted ice cream. To our amazement, he dropped the coin at my feet and waited for his reward.

Another time, when I was 24, we tested Tarzan's natural protective instincts. Jack, then 15, and Carl, 14, tied my hands behind

GOOD DOG. Tarzan posed with his masters, the author (kneeling) and his brothers, in their New Jersey hometown in 1936. Carl (far left) and Jack are holding their other pets, which happened to be cats. Tarzan did his best to ignore them.

my back with clothesline and left me on the floor in the kitchen.

Then they excitedly asked Tarzan to go find me. He did, and when he saw me "struggling" to get free, he whined and licked my face. I showed him my tied wrists and waited to see what he'd do.

Tarzan to the Rescue!

I was more than surprised when the dog carefully put his head sideways on my arm, got the rope between his powerful incisors and cut through the rope in three bites!

As time passed, Tarzan learned many more tricks and never failed to amaze us with his intelligence.

Then along came World War II. Jack and Carl enlisted and left home, and Tarzan grieved for days, periodically visiting their bedrooms and resting his head on their beds.

We felt he'd soon forget the boys, as we'd heard a dog's memory lasted only about six weeks. The boys were in the service for about 2½ years, and Carl was the first to come home.

When Carl arrived in his Army uniform, Tarzan growled, as he would at any stranger, and shunned Carl's attempt to pet him. He was told to lie in his bed under the sink, which he did, but he still kept up a low-level growl.

About half an hour later, as Carl was telling us about his experiences in the war, Tarzan sprang from his bed and lunged at him! For a moment we were horrified, but when Tarzan started to whine and lick Carl's face, we knew he'd finally remembered Carl. For the next few days, they were inseparable.

Tarzan was 16 when he died—it's said that equates to about 112 in terms of human age. Afterward, my parents adopted other dogs of the same breed…but there never was another Tarzan.

pony on parade

My parents rode horses, which they showed off in many local parades. As a 7-year-old boy in 1938, I was thrilled when Mom and Dad bought me my own pony. Puggy and I became the best of pals, and he followed me around outside just like a puppy. One day, we were getting ready to attend a parade. My parents loaded the horse trailer and opened the back door of our Buick so I could get in. Being the loyal pal he was, Puggy climbed in next to me and stuck his head out the window. He seemed so happy that we didn't have the heart to leave him behind. So off we went! From that time on, whenever we appeared in a parade, so did Puggy.

— *Gene Bunch, Placerville, California*

10

Growing Up

parakeets were keen

parakeet versus vacuum

Back in the late 1950s, when I was about 9 years old, we had a little blue parakeet named Quito. A chore I really despised was cleaning his cage. One day I decided to take a shortcut. I pulled out my mother's Electrolux canister vacuum, attached the hose, opened the cage and vacuumed up the debris, much to the consternation of the poor bird.

Suddenly I heard a strange noise and realized Quito was no longer on his perch. In fact, he was no longer in the cage! After switching off the vacuum and falling to my knees, I frantically began pulling dirt out of the canister. Before long, a little ball of dust came staggering out of the Electrolux. Quito had survived! He hopped a few steps and stopped. Then he began sneezing, a tiny cloud of dust escaping from him each time.

Happily, Quito lived many years, and I resigned myself to cleaning his cage by hand. But he became a little agitated every time someone turned on the vacuum cleaner!

—*Margy Ashley*
Canandaigua, New York

PET PALS. "We had a 2-year-old parakeet, Pete, when we acquired our cocker spaniel, Fluff," writes Millie McNair, La Grange Park, Illinois. "The dog loved to play with Pete's toys, although Pete was a little selfish and he'd sometimes peck Fluff on the nose. But when Pete was in a good mood, he'd give Fluff a loud kiss on the nose instead. A few days after we got Fluff, we heard Pete whine exactly like the puppy did."

PRETTY BIRD. Like the girls in this photo, Margy Ashley of Canandaigua, New York, had a pet parakeet that provided hours of no-frills fun. The photo is from Linnea Danielson of Minneapolis.

kids are crazy for canines

A DOLL OF A DOG. "My older sister, Barbara, and I were thrilled when our parents brought home Spot," says Janet Loewe of Clarks Summit, Pennsylvania. "He was very well behaved and quite tolerant of us treating him like a living doll. Here, in 1939, we dressed him up and took him for rides in our pedal car."

TUCKERED OUT. "Our son Bruce, then 2, was using his pal Cherie for a pillow," recalls Odette Landers of Fort Pierce, Florida. "My husband, Bill, took this slide on the stoop of our house in Hauppauge, New York, in the early '60s."

JUST LIKE LASSIE. "When our son, Gordon, was born in 1961, we feared our collie, Duchess, would be jealous," recalls Florence Clay of Bokeelia, Florida. "Just the opposite was true. Duchess was the proud protector of Gordon, as seen here when Gordon was 6 months old. The two were ready for our daily trip to the post office in Ocean Gate, New Jersey."

PAL FLOCKED TO CHICKENS

When I was 6, I traveled with my parents and my brother, Larry, on a hot, dusty, overcrowded troop train from Caldwell, Idaho, to Albany, Oregon, to begin a new life on a small acreage.

World War II was in full swing, and times were hard. Because gas was rationed, my father rode a bicycle to and from the jobs he took in town.

The following summer, 1943, Dad came home with a surprise. Nestled in his bicycle basket was a black-and-white puppy. Someone in town had an unwanted litter, and free was just the right price for us.

Upon Mom's insistence, Pal was strictly an outdoor dog. But he didn't seem to mind one bit. Dad built a snug shelter on the back porch so Pal was always warm and comfy, even in winter. He seemed to enjoy the company of our cow, horse, cats and pigs.

But Pal took a particular interest in our chickens. He never chased them; he merely circled them from time to time, with an occasional low growl to warn them if they were wandering too far afield.

Sometimes our neighbor's chickens would escape and head over to see what tasty tidbits our brood was pecking and scratching at. We never figured out how Pal knew which chickens were ours and which ones were the intruders, but he always managed to detect the fugitive fowl and send them packing.

For years, Pal was a treasured member of our family, not to mention a furry farmhand!

—*Betty Davis, Salem, Oregon*

BROTHERLY LOVE. Nine-year-old Donald Parks of Allentown, Pennsylvania, became the happiest kid in the world when his brother surprised him with a beagle puppy named Bo in 1949. Bo was Donald's companion for 10 years.

CAN-DO CANINE
OVERCAME DISABILITY

One day in 1927, my dad brought home a squirming bundle of fur that turned out to be a purebred German shepherd puppy, the runt of the litter. Since police often used this breed, we naturally named him Koppy.

My parents' business was breeding and selling collies, and Koppy became the leader of the pack. All the dogs loved him, especially the puppies.

Koppy's worst habit was chasing cars. One day he failed to show up for dinner, so my mother went looking for him. Koppy had indeed "caught" one of the cars and was badly injured. The vet said there were two options: remove his injured leg or put him down. But Koppy had won over my collie-loving mother,

who said, "There's no choice. Remove the leg." The loss of the leg slowed Koppy down, but only momentarily. He continued to reign over the dogs at our kennel and even led the daily exercise runs up in our fields—after I gave him a bit of a head start.

As a house dog, Koppy had privileges our kennel dogs did not. For instance, on Sunday morning—and only on Sunday morning—Koppy waited by the breakfast table until someone left, and then he would take over the vacant chair. We tucked a napkin under his collar and placed a breakfast treat in front of him. Koppy would happily lap up his breakfast, get down from the chair and leave the room. He was a true original.

—*Dick Lawton, Zellwood, Florida*

PUPPY LOVE.
"This is our daughter Shan and the family's puppy in 1958," relates A.E. Briggs from Austin, Texas. "The photograph was taken at our home in Atlanta, Georgia."

BEWARE THE DOG. "My dog, Patsy, was very protective of me," Beatrice Lehman Henriott of Knox, Indiana, relates. "If anyone approached pretending to harm me, Patsy would growl and bare her teeth. This picture, taken in 1932 at our home in Wakarusa, Indiana, was labeled 'guard duty.'"

The dog was created specially for children. He is the god of frolic.

—HENRY WARD BEECHER

PET EXPRESS. "My youngest brother, Don, loved to play with our dog and the kittens on our dad's farm near Duncan, Nebraska," writes Doris Lemp Melliger of Columbus. "He spent most of his summer vacation hauling them around. His older three brothers had to help with chores, so he entertained himself. Mother took this picture in 1948. Note the homemade side boards and the kittens with the dog."

Precious Pets

NOW! A DRY DOG FOOD DESIGNED FOR
FASTER, EASIER MIXING!

NEW FRISKIES MIX: *Mixes faster, easier with water, milk, gravy, canned dog food or left-overs!*

Special absorbent texture is the secret of new Friskies Mix! Each morsel soaks up and holds whatever liquid you add, allows perfect blending with canned dog foods, fresh meat or wholesome left-overs! Quickly, completely—without tiresome stirring, Friskies Mix blends into a tasty deluxe meal!

Tastes great fed dry, too, because of Friskies crunchy texture and natural flavor. Any way you serve it, Friskies Mix is fully nourishing...perfectly balanced, with all the vitamins, minerals and protein your dog is known to need for top condition, growth, energy. Treat *your* dog to Friskies Mix. *Another quality pet food from* Carnation.

***Another new dog food* – FRISKIES MAGIC SAUCE CUBES!**
Amazing new taste discovery—makes its own tasty sauce like magic— seconds after you add water! Tastes great fed dry, too. Fully nourishing.

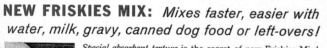

1963

we found a warrior in our 'watchdog'

by Neel Summers, Holmesville, Ohio

During the Great Depression, our family of six survived by subsistence farming on my uncle's small hillside farm in Wallback, West Virginia. When we were free from our farm chores, my three brothers and I had great times roaming the nearby fields and woods. Our fun was enhanced in the spring of 1935 after my older brother brought home a yellow puppy named Watch.

Watch became a tireless, eager hunter, which helped us get much-needed wild game for the dinner table. During our hunting excursions, my brothers and I acquired pelts, which we sold for a few precious dollars each.

Our brother named the puppy with the idea that he would become a good watchdog. Watch met that expectation in spades. On one occasion, his protective instincts surely saved me and my mother from serious injury.

The advent of World War II required my father to work at an Ohio defense plant and took my older brother to Europe. As a 12-year-old boy, I was my mother's chief helper with farm chores and with the care of my two younger brothers.

We had a cantankerous milk cow, aptly named Old Horny, with a wicked set of horns and a disposition to match. She had severely gored Watch when he was a pup, and as an adult, he gleefully repaid her whenever she got out of line!

He Didn't Cower from Bull

One day in the summer of 1943, Old Horny disappeared from our pasture. My mother surmised that she had escaped to visit a bull half a mile away. Sure enough, we found Old Horny with the bull high on a hill in his pasture. When we tried to drive Old Horny away from the herd, the bull—taking offense at losing the newest member of his harem—snorted loudly and charged us. My mother and I were caught defenseless in the open field, but Watch met the bull's charge head-on.

When the bull lowered his head in an attempt to gore him, Watch sank his teeth into the soft flesh of the animal's nose and held on tight. With a violent shake, the bull sent Watch flying. After a hard landing, Watch bounced right back up and went on the attack again, this time grabbing the bull's tail. Bellowing and kicking, the bull took off running toward his barnyard nearly a quarter mile away, with Watch hanging on tenaciously.

Still shaken, my mother and I followed, fearing for the fate of our protector. But we need not have worried. When the barnyard came into sight, we saw the bull—bloody and beaten—standing docilely in a corner, with Watch standing in front of him as if daring the bull to attack again.

After returning Old Horny to our own barn, I rewarded Watch with many hugs—and Mom surprised him with his favorite treat, a huge slice of her homemade cornbread.

Precious Pets

17

animals captured the hearts of audiences

Not only did pets play an important part in our childhoods, they also had starring roles in beloved children's television programs. All kinds of animals served as proud protectors, trusty sidekicks and loyal friends—just like cherished pets in real life.

The Lone Ranger — 1949–1957

"Heigh-ho, Silver, away!" With that command, the Lone Ranger's mighty white stallion was off, carrying his master wherever injustice raised its head on the frontier of the Old West. Cattle thieves, crooked land dealers, highwaymen—they didn't stand a chance against the masked man and his gallant steed. Always at the ready, this impressive equine waited just long enough for his master to leap into the saddle, then galloped away to fight lawlessness and keep peaceful settlers safe. What fun for viewers to go along with this heroic horse as he thundered across the plains!

The Adventures of Rin Tin Tin — 1954–1959

A young boy and his German shepherd puppy were the lone survivors when Indians attacked their wagon train. Rescued by the U.S. Cavalry, the orphan and his dog remained at Fort Apache as honorary troopers. And no more dedicated troopers were there than Cpl. Rusty and Pvt. Rin Tin Tin. Led by Lt. Rip Masters, these "pals through thick and thin" were inseparable as they helped establish law and order in the Old West. Whether retrieving lifesaving medicine or fighting desperadoes, Rin Tin Tin proved just as worthy of his rank as his human comrades.

Lassie — 1954–1974

The name alone conjures up the image of a beautiful long-haired collie standing majestically on a hilltop. Beginning as a beloved family pet before venturing out on her own toward the end of the series, this four-legged phenom had an amazing ability to sniff out danger and save the day. Kids on the show had a knack for getting into trouble, but no situation was too daunting for Lassie. Whether Timmy was threatened by a bear, stuck in a live minefield, trapped in a badger hole or caught in an earthquake, one call of "Laaasssieee!" and help was on the way.

The Little Rascals — 1955

Spanky, Buckwheat, Alfalfa—the young scamps originally known as Our Gang just weren't complete without Petey the Pup. This lovable pit bull with the trademark ring around his eye was as devoted a pooch as could be. Whether doing tricks, rescuing a swimmer, chasing away bad guys or catching a flyaway kite, he was always beside his friends. And the kids loved him right back. When a shopkeeper told the youngsters they could have a toy in exchange for Petey, one replied defiantly, "I wouldn't trade that dog for your whole darn store!"

Fury — 1955–1960

On the surface, a big wild horse "full of fire and fury" doesn't seem like the best choice for a pet. But this untamed equine soon mellowed after orphan Joey came to live with Jim Newton at the Broken Wheel Ranch. Fury learned to love the child, and Joey became the only human Fury would respond to. The "king of the wild stallions," this free-spirited horse extended his power and strength to the small boy, and Joey rode him on many adventures, learning valuable lessons along the way.

Mister Ed — 1961–1966

This personable Palomino was probably the most human of all TV pets—and not just because he could talk. In different episodes, he was an artist, baseball player, entrepreneur, game show winner, truck driver, pilot, surfer—even a secret agent! His favorite pastime was making mischief, from dialing up prank phone calls to tunneling out of his stall. But at the end of the day, he was always a buddy to his owner. Wilbur was the only human Mister Ed liked enough to speak with face to face—and Wilbur liked Mister Ed enough to keep him around despite the disapproval of his wife.

Flipper — 1964–1967

A marine mammal can make the perfect sidekick—when you live on the Florida coast. The gentle, precocious dolphin they called Flipper showed unwavering loyalty to his companions, especially young Bud. And this smart cetacean kept things swingin' at the Coral Key Park & Marine Reserve. His entertaining water tricks delighted children, and his squeaks and whistles somehow communicated volumes to his human friends. Plus, this bottlenose buddy was always there to help swimmers in distress. After watching Flipper, your pet goldfish just didn't seem the same.

* That's quite a prize you have there, bright eyes. And a pretty picture you make with that colorful yarn and that wide-eyed look. That's how it is with Puss 'N Boots Cats... the Vitamin A gives their eyes sparkle, so makes them extra lovable...
* Where'd you get that silky, luxurious fur coat? From a Puss 'N Boots can, you say? That's a point! Puss 'N Boots is rich in riboflavin, one of the important nutrients you need to keep your skin healthy—your fur fluffy and full.
* Nice kitty! Takes more than a tangle with a ball of yarn to upset your gentle disposition. Thank Puss 'N Boots for the part it plays. It's so rich in nerve-soothing Vitamin B1, it would help tame even a battle-scarred Tom!
PUSS'N BOOTS
REG. U.S. PAT. OFF.
CAT FOOD
This yarn's for you, my pretties!
* My what strong bones you have! The better to leap with, of course. It's easy to see you're getting lots of calcium, phosphorus, and Vitamin D. That's no surprise with Puss 'N Boots on your diet. There's a dish worth leaping for!
See what it means...* to be a Puss 'N Boots Cat?
©1951, Coast Fishing Co. Wilmington Calif.
* Hey! You're missing the fun! Or are you... Isn't that Puss 'N Boots? 'Nuff said!
Yes, all you purry, furry pals have lots in common... health, energy, beauty, and a love for Puss 'N Boots. That's natural, for Puss 'N Boots is finest quality. Fresh-caught whole fish (no by-products or "fillers" ever) plus just the right cereals, cooked in the can and ready to eat. Each feeding of Puss 'N Boots gives you all the food factors found in milk, liver, salmon, and beef... in greater abundance and even better balance. Yet Puss 'N Boots costs your master and mistress far less!
Puss 'N Boots adds the Plus!
QUALITY MAKES IT... AMERICA'S LARGEST SELLING CAT FOOD

1951

family's feline friend

"Our daughter Diane was all dressed up for her birthday when this slide was taken in 1959," remembers Corinne Ramage of Omaha, Nebraska. "She's holding the family feline, Sam."

NOW SPELL "CAT."

"This is my son, Peter, and our cat, Tippie, named for the white tip on his tail when he was a kitten," says Irene Powell of Des Moines, Washington. "My husband took this photo, which we used for our Christmas card in 1947. Tippie was very smart. We had him for 15 years."

fun on the farm

FARM LIFE WAS HARD WORK, BUT IT GAVE KIDS A CHANCE TO HAVE AN ASSORTMENT OF PETS AT THE READY!

WHOA, NELLIE! "Growing up in rural Kansas during the 1930s, my greatest joy was riding our sorrel mare, Nellie," recalls Sally Baldwin of Arroyo Grande, California. "My younger brother, Rex, and I often rode Nellie bareback to town for groceries, to bring the cows in for milking and to visit nearby relatives."

RIDE 'EM, PIGBOY. "My brother, Bill McCaleb, wanted a pony," explains Lela Budwine of Lake Jackson, Texas. "Since he couldn't have one, he settled for Eagle, our pet hog. These two had great fun together, and Bill would happily ride Eagle for hours."

THREE PETS, TWO SHOES.
"My brothers Roger (left) and Adolph Svejkovsky posed with their pets on our grandfather's farm outside London, Minnesota, in 1928," relates Lucille Moore of Austin. "I was 10 at the time. The sheep was Blackie, the dog Snoopy and the cat Kitty. I found the picture among my mother's treasures when she died in 1996 at the age of 100."

CHICK 'N' LITTLE. "This precious scene shows my son, Roger, holding a yellow chick," says Ross Dornbush of Jenison, Michigan. "I bought about 100 of them to raise. The kids were enthralled with their fluffy friends!"

CALF-ING FUN.
"Living on a farm during the 1950s, we were always short on money, but not imagination," writes Bill Kiehn of Marlow, Oklahoma. "My sister Phyllis (pictured here with cousins Ronny and Joe Kiehn) and I broke this orphaned calf to ride and to carry our equipment to our hideout in the pasture."

BUNNY BUDDIES.
Margaret Schulz of Salina, Kansas, snapped this photo of her son Mike, 7, and daughter Marilyn, 2, in 1956. At the time, the family raised and sold white rabbits, and the kids couldn't resist playing with them.

oinker made her break at the fair

By Carol Fellin, Oconomowoc, Wisconsin

I was a 10-year-old feminist in 1955, although I didn't know it. I didn't want to do a "girlish" 4-H project like sewing or cooking. I wanted to raise a pig and enter it in the Dodge County (Wisconsin) Fair instead.

My parents were freethinkers and allowed me to raise a purebred Poland China pig. How I loved caring for that little oinker. The fact that I was the only girl at the project meetings only made it more fun.

Showing the pig at the fair proved to be a bit more of a dilemma. The boys stayed overnight in the barn to keep their eyes on their pigs and have a good time. Even my parents weren't liberal enough to allow that, so I brought my pig to the fair on the morning of the show from our farm in the township of Ashippun.

Our method of transporting the pig was a bit unorthodox. We crammed her in a wooden slatted box so tightly, it was like fitting a hand into a glove. Then my father placed the crate in the trunk of our car, and off we went.

I wasn't well equipped for the show ring, either. All the boys showing their pigs had fancy canes to guide their animals around; I just had a stick I found on the ground.

I guess it wasn't a big surprise when I received the last-place ribbon.

After the fair ended, my father went up to get my pig while I was back at school. Dad loaded her in the same wooden crate, but this time, my fine swine chose to inhale, and the box burst wide open. Realizing she was free, the pig ran lickety-split across the fairgrounds with my dad running close behind.

Being no fool, the pig ran into the one place Dad couldn't chase her—the ladies' restroom. Dad stood outside as several women came running out, telling him what he already knew: "There's a pig in there!"

Dad did the practical thing. He pounded a few more nails into the wooden box, trapped the pig and put her back into the crate. He placed her in the car trunk and drove home.

Well, she had her shot at being a county fair queen, but back on the farm, she ate her feed on all fours, just like the rest of our cherished barnyard animals.

PIG GOES HOG WILD. Both the author and her Poland China pig had minds of their own, which was all right at the farm, but at the county fair, it meant no ribbons.

dad couldn't bear to leave cub behind

On a trip to Canada in 1938, Dad came across a bear cub whose mother had been killed by hunters. Dad loved animals and just couldn't abandon the cub to fend for itself. With border patrol being more easygoing in those days, he brought Tillie home to Iowa for me to raise.

Tillie played like a puppy and even wore a dog harness. I loved walking her on a leash through the streets of town, which made people stop and stare before slowly approaching for a closer look. On weekends, Tillie went with the family to our cottage on Cedar River. At first she was leery of the water, but eventually she learned the dog paddle.

Although Tillie was friendly with everyone, she loved my dad the most and would welcome him home by jumping on him. It didn't take long for Tillie to grow from a cuddly cub to a good-size gal.

With her paws on Dad's shoulders, they were eye to eye, and her greetings were now knocking Dad to the ground. Soon Tillie's full-grown size made her loving and playing too much to handle, and she had to go.

Luckily, a zoo in Cedar Rapids offered to take Tillie in. She adapted easily to her new life and even had cubs of her own. Whenever we went to visit, Tillie came to the bars so Dad could pet her. We never forgot about Tillie—and, clearly, she never forgot about us.

—*Connie Roth, Rocklin, California*

HIS PET WAS JUST DUCKY.
"This is my son, John Henry, and his pet mallard, Irving, in 1960," relates Jeanne LaFrenier of Lunenburg, Massachusetts. "We picked up the duck when it started following us while we were bicycling at Cape Cod. We took it home, where Irving became a pet and lived for seven years."

26

HANDLE WITH KID GLOVES. "I took this slide of my nephew Jim Hough in 1953," says Ken Geyer of Marion, Ohio. "A baby squirrel had fallen out of its nest, and Jim cared for it until it was big enough to go back into the wild."

one-trick pony?

Skeeter was a small dapple-gray mare my two older brothers and I used for fun and transportation when we were growing up near Kittitas, Washington. Skeeter (shown with me at right) had a mind of her own, as my brother Bob found out on his first trip.

We always took the shortest route to town when we had a nickel to spend for candy at Ernie Divines' general store. The route went across a field and through a creek.

In the middle of the creek, Skeeter would pull on the reins as if she wanted a drink. But the rider who gave in soon found himself in the drink, as Skeeter would flop over in the water and dump the rider.

Of course, Skeeter's little trick was withheld from the next rider. As a result, nearly every Skeeter rider ended up being dunked. What fun!

—*Donald Sorenson, Ellensburg, Washington*

Precious Pets

clementine got our goat

As a teenager in the 1930s, I received a most unusual pet from a boyfriend. Clementine was a white kid goat with a pink nose and pretty blue eyes. But her innocent appearance was a disguise. Clementine was a little bundle of dynamite.

No matter how securely we tied her up in the yard, Clementine would break free. One spring afternoon, she took a stroll on our wraparound porch to investigate the Ladies' Aid Society meeting my mother was hosting in the living room. The windows were wide open to catch the fresh breeze, and Clementine took that as an invitation to join the meeting. As the ladies ate cake and drank coffee, Clementine nibbled away on Mother's lace curtains.

The mischief that cemented Clementine's future, however, involved my brother Bayard. He had just painstakingly stacked firewood to last us through the winter. Clementine got the idea that the 4-foot-high, 20-foot-long structure was meant for her entertainment. Up she climbed—and down came the wood. That was it. Dad found a farmer to take her off our hands.

Some time later, the new owner came by with a special remembrance of Clementine—twin white goats with pink noses and blue eyes. We all agreed they were adorable—but for someone else to enjoy!

—*Virginia Buxton, Jonesborough, Tennessee*

A BOY AND HIS DOG...AND HIS RABBIT?

When Roger Magner, his dog, Pepper, and his rabbit, Muffin, went for a walk in May of 1958, Roger did most of the walking.

This boyhood scene was shared by Roger's mom, Hazel Magner, of Omaha, Nebraska. "Pepper would ride piggyback by putting his back paws on Roger's belt and his front paws on Roger's shoulders," she explains. "Pepper was jealous, so when my son started carrying Muffin, the dog figured out how to come along for the ride!

"Pepper also envied our pet bird," adds Hazel. "Whenever Roger went up to the cage to talk to the bird, Pepper jumped up on a nearby footstool so he could get in on the conversation."

sizing up the pumpkin prospects

My mother told me this photo was taken by a traveling photographer in about 1940, when I was 10. I don't really remember it, but that's me out in our pumpkin patch in Tomah, Wisconsin, with my dog, Tippy. He was a constant companion and always followed me to the one-room school on our farm.

—*Douglas Randall, Beaver Dam, Wisconsin*

CHAPTER TWO

Road Trip!

From outings with Dad and simple Sunday drives to trips across town and vacations to other states, kids are thrilled anytime they have a chance to leave home. After all, no one knows just what adventures await them on the open road!

"On the heels of a major snowstorm in 1939, nine members of my family traveled from Kansas to my grandfather's boyhood home in Illinois," recalls Opal Jones of Mayfield, Kansas. "Dad's Ford pickup had just one bench seat and no topper, so he built a wooden frame over the truck bed and covered it with a canvas tarp to protect us from the wind and cold.

"As Dad drove, Grandpa would occasionally raise the flap so we could view the beauty of the snow-covered landscape. It looked like a fairy tale to my 7-year-old eyes! At each filling station stop, we'd hop out and huddle around the ever-present coal- or wood-burning potbellied stove. Oh, how good that felt!

"Kids today would find it hard to believe that this was an exciting and happy time. But as we rode along, we sang songs, told stories and made memories for our family."

Settle back and take an armchair trip with other folks who share their heartwarming, harrowing and often hilarious journeys.

dad's vacation 'bug'

By Florence Burden
Torrington, Wyoming

When Dad suggested a family vacation in our 1925 Model T touring car, we had high hopes. Both Mom and Dad and my two sisters were happy and optimistic when we started out that summer of 1929.

We'd never taken a long trip before. Now we were going to drive 400 miles—from Scottsbluff, Nebraska, east to Grandma's farm in Antelope County.

I was 10 years old, and my sisters were 12 and 14. For the trip, Mom bought each of us girls khaki pants—the latest fad. They came just below the knee and buttoned with a flap. We were very proud of them, even if Dad teased us about our "new look."

With good weather the first two days, we enjoyed stopping for gas at the filling stations that had soda pop cooling in tubs of ice. Dad would buy us all a 5-cent bottle of pop and we'd have to drink it right away and leave the bottle there.

One station had a sign that read, "We don't know where Mom is, but we have Pop on ice." We laughed and laughed at that one.

On the third day, we woke early, had a quick breakfast of cornflakes, milk, doughnuts and bananas. With the mattress rolled and tied to the back of the Ford, we set out through the Nebraska Sandhills toward Grandma's.

We noticed motorists waving as they passed—some were even yelling and pointing. When Dad stopped to let the radiator cool, we found out why.

Bedding Left Behind

What was left of the mattress was dragging along the road. No wonder people had been pointing at us!

We arrived safely at Grandma's and were happy to sleep in real beds and eat good food for a week. For the trip home, Grandma gave us another mattress and a basket of goodies.

The sky was cloudy as we drove toward our campsite in Valentine on the first

ROAD REGRETS. Florence Burden (right) was excited about the family's first car trip, but her parents' enthusiasm dimmed as time went on.

night. A bad storm was brewing and, by late afternoon, Mom was begging Dad not to set up the tent.

Why not rent a tourist cabin near the campgrounds? Dad said it would cost too much money. When the storm hit—complete with hail—it was impossible to build a campfire, so we ate the food Grandma had sent and went to bed.

We fell asleep with the storm still raging—and woke a short time later when the tent blew down on top of us! Scrambling out from under it, we made our way back to the car.

Silence Was Deafening

Everyone was wet and unhappy. Grabbing me by the hand, Mom informed Dad she was taking me to find a hotel room. We walked the half-mile to town (by the time we checked in, we were soaking wet). Meanwhile, Dad and my sisters spent a very soggy night in the car.

Next morning, we all went to a cafe for a hot breakfast, then set out for Marsland (where Dad's sister lived). By then, Dad and Mom were barely speaking to one another.

Dad said it wasn't his fault it had rained. Mom didn't answer because she still had a headache from where the pole hit her when the tent blew down. At this point, we girls knew better than to talk or sing.

After two days at Aunt Sadie's, we drove home. As we unloaded the Model T, I heard Dad say to Mom, "Don't ask me to go on any more vacations." And Mom assured him she didn't ever want another trip like that one.

It was the only family vacation we ever took. I guess once was enough!

Follow Highway 58 from Chattanooga, Tenn. Up Lookout Mountain to Rock City

ROCKY WALK ON LOOKOUT MOUNTAIN

After spying See Rock City painted on top of barns throughout the South for years, I was thrilled when my family decided to stop there on our way back from North Carolina in 1960. Just outside Chattanooga, Tennesee, Rock City sits on top of Lookout Mountain, where tourists get a view of seven states. The most exciting thing for me (I was 12 years old then) was the swinging bridge over a valley. While my dad and sister walked carefully to avoid too much movement, I ran full steam ahead. My sister never let me live that down!

—*Danny Atchley*
Mineral Wells, Texas

THE BEAUTY OF THE BLACK HILLS

EARLY VISITOR TO THE AREA. The summer of 1927 was an important time in the Black Hills of South Dakota. President Coolidge arrived for a three-week vacation and liked the area so much that he stayed for three months. Gutzon Borglum was hired to begin the drilling and sculpting on Mount Rushmore.

A profitable tourist industry was growing stronger with every news story about the wonders of an area being called "the richest 100 square miles on the face of the earth."

So many people visited the area and wanted to climb its highest mountain, Harney Peak, that crude ladders were erected and a lookout built. I was 3 when I climbed it with my dad. We went all the way to the top!
—*Ari Jones, Rapid City, South Dakota*

PHOTO OP. "We took this slide of our boys, Gerry (left) and Clay, at Mount Rushmore with a costumed Native American," recalls Jean St. Pierre of Tiverton, Rhode Island. "We stopped at the national memorial in 1962."

SEEING THE SIGHTS. A summer vacation to South Dakota was a frequent adventure for families, including Carol Sieborg's of Omaha. "During a stop at Custer State Park in 1968, the friendly donkeys came to say hello and to beg for food. My son Steven decided to keep his hands to himself, while daughter Susan and I (in sunglasses) looked on," writes Carol.

MOTORING MEMORIES

Long before planes became the preferred mode of travel, folks hopped in their cars and hit the road for fun and frolics.

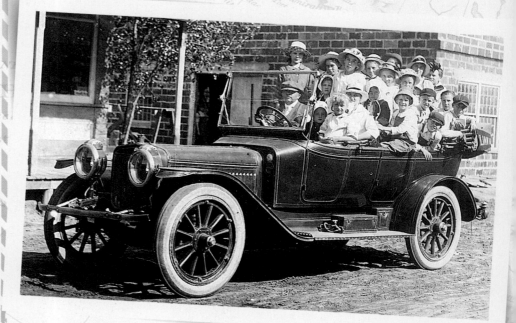

uncle's winton packed in the picnic bunch

In the spring of 1916, when I was in first grade in Linn, Kansas, my uncle was driving a 1909 Winton.

As the end of the school year approached, our teacher informed us that our annual last-day-of-school picnic would probably have to be held on the school grounds.

Normally the picnic was held along a creek a couple miles outside of town, but the man who usually furnished his hayrack for this auspicious event was not able to help us this year.

So I took it upon myself to tell the teacher my uncle would be glad to take us. Fortunately, when I told him about my unsolicited offer, he was flattered.

When the big day finally came, about 25 excited youngsters (everyone in grades one through four!) were packed into that Winton. For many of them, it was their first automobile ride ever.

—*Naomi Richwine*
Lincoln, Nebraska

ILLINOIS TO IOWA. Mildred Blaum (right) and her sister were along for the ride to their grandparents' house when a little brother's toy nearly gave their dad a heart attack, as she explains in the story below. The car shown in this photo belonged to Mildred's grandparents.

COLE

139313

'whistle stop' nearly did dad in

After my Grandpa and Grandma Marshall moved from Illinois to a farm near Klemme, Iowa, we didn't get to see them as often as we had when they lived in the next county. So, when Papa bought our first car, a 1917 Model T, we made plans to drive out to visit them.

All of Mother's family lived in Iowa, so she was eager to see them. But first, she bought some little things at the dime store for us kids to play with during our two-day trip.

However, her choice for my little brother, John, was not one of her better ideas. Being a new driver, Papa was concentrating mightily on his driving and was far from relaxed. Just as we came to a railroad crossing, Johnny decided to try out his new whistle.

Poor Papa! Thinking a train was bearing down on us, he slammed on the brakes, then made a right-hand sweep up along the side of the tracks. Needless to say, that was the end of that whistle.

Although it about scared Papa to death, it sure made for a great family story in the years to come.

—*Mildred Blaum, New Holland, Illinois*

where's the kitchen sink?

This 1961 photo from Noreen Collier of Jackson, Michigan, proves things haven't changed much when packing for a long family vacation. Her family's car is loaded with all the necessities for a stay at the South Kawishiwi River Campground in northern Minnesota.

Go Places on Kellys

"Kellys are Tough!"

IT'S GOODBYE FUN when a tired old tire collapses on a lonely road. It's worse—much worse—when a smooth tread slips on wet pavement.

Before your next motor trip, put on a set of tough new Kelly Tires—have the most sensible kind of safety insurance on all four wheels. Then you can forget your tire troubles. Kellys will carry you faithfully, silently, safely mile after mile...day after day...season after season.

That **Armorubber** Tread answers a vital need of today's driving. It gives Kellys a tough, close-textured riding surface that stays safe extra thousands of miles...literally outwears the toughest steel!

Can you afford Kellys? Yes...easily. Their low cost—only a few dimes per 1000 miles—will fit neatly into your present car-upkeep budget. Drive in and talk trade with your friendly, nearby Kelly dealer today.

1939

a 1,000-mile trip ...and no blowouts!

By Leslie Hauger, Tulsa, Oklahoma

In 1912, my father bought a new Cadillac, the first model with electric lights and starter. Our first big trip was from our home in Louisville, Kentucky, to a Michigan resort.

My uncle, aunt and their daughter rode along. We planned to spend the first night in Indianapolis, a little over 100 miles away.

There were no road maps or marked highways. We had something called a "Blue Book." Uncle Doc turned to the page that said "Louisville to Indianapolis" and read:

"Drive north on Spring Street for 9 and 2/10 miles. Jog east for 2½ miles, then turn north past white farmhouse on southwest corner..."

Soon the road dead-ended at a river. There was no bridge, but Mother spotted a ferry anchored on the far bank. We assumed the ferryman lived in the nearby house, so my dad and Uncle Doc got out and started to yell. There was no response.

After many shouts and still no answer, Uncle Doc lost patience. He got out a revolver and fired two shots in the air.

A chubby lady scurried onto the porch and yelled, "He's eatin' his dinner and will be out when he's done!"

He didn't saunter out for a while. Uncle Doc held his temper as we were ferried across the river and paid the 50-cent fee.

When it started to rain, the car got stuck in a mud hole. A farmer came out of his house and offered to pull us out—for $5.

Uncle Doc grumbled, "I do believe that man dug out this hole just so motorists would get stuck." It was a good thing he'd put his revolver back in the car!

While we made it to Indianapolis before dark, we didn't get to Michigan the next afternoon because the car quit running and couldn't be fixed until the following day.

Two weeks later, after a wonderful vacation, we rolled back home. We'd made a 1,000-mile round-trip without one blowout!

A "NON-TIRING" TRIP. Leslie Hauger's family got their picture in the local paper after their punctureless 1,000-mile drive in 1912. That's Leslie at left, mugging for the camera.

HAND-TO-MOUTH MOMENT. "During a trip to the Grand Canyon in 1966, my son, John, and daughter, Patty, were greeted by friendly squirrels," recalls Joan Backus of Prescott, Arizona. Looks as if the kids had the critters eating out of their hands.

ONLY YOU KNOW WHO. "When the kids were growing up, we camped frequently," says Barbara Moellering, Rock Island, Illinois. "During a campout at Scott County Park near Davenport, Iowa, our daughters—Barb, 10; Judy, 8; and Cheryl, almost 6—met up with Smokey Bear. As a family of conservationists, it was a moment to remember."

thanks for the memories

ROUTE 66 LED TO ADVENTURE. "In June 1960, we drove from New Jersey to California on old Route 66," says Elwood Taylor, Mount Ephraim, New Jersey. "On a stop at the Petrified Forest, our 3-year-old son, Tom, enjoyed a rest." Tom's red tennis shoes were a fashion statement.

SAY "CHEESE!" Corinne Ramage of Omaha, Nebraska, captured this photo of kids Mark and Diane in Estes Park, Colorado, around 1956. Mark's T-shirt pays homage to Wyatt Earp, his hero at the time.

slumming in the chevy

A meal at a high-class hotel was a humbling experience.

By Dick Woollen, North Hollywood, California

One of my father's greatest pleasures was planning extended summer driving trips out to the Western states.

He was partially paralyzed while serving in the Navy during World War I, so he enlisted his friend, Harold Noyes, to help my mother with the driving. We crammed our 1932 maroon Chevy with luggage and set off.

We typically stopped for the night at shacklike cabins and the occasional hotel. But one day, Dad decided we should sample the lifestyle of the rich and famous by stopping at the elegant Broadmoor Hotel in Colorado Springs. The dignified doorman at the entrance pretended it wasn't unusual for the Broadmoor clientele to have luggage strapped to the roof of a dusty old Chevy.

Mind you, we weren't planning anything as extravagant as an overnight stay, just a special meal in the dining room. When we entered it, I was awestruck by the marble pillars and floor and the elegant couples dancing to the music of the orchestra.

We were seated and studied the menus intensely. There was a long moment of silence as the four of us exchanged glances. The menu was written in French. Waiters had surrounded us, awaiting our orders, but we were frozen. Just as Dad started to giggle, Harold saved the day by deciding that *rosbif* sounded good. We all ordered the same.

Throughout the roast beef dinner, I had the uncomfortable feeling that the ever-lurking waiters did not approve of my table manners, especially as I attempted to eat a slippery peeled peach that had been maliciously served on a flat plate.

While Dad waited for the change from the waiter, we decided to view the artwork in the dining room. As our waiter was heading back to our table, Dad waved at him to indicate where we were. The waiter waved back, smiled and continued right to the kitchen with a hefty tip in hand

The dignified doorman at the entrance pretended it wasn't unusual for the Broadmoor clientele to have luggage strapped to the roof of a dusty old Chevy.

As a courtesy when the doorman brought us our car, he tried to turn on the interior dome light, but it wouldn't go on. Embarrassed, we climbed in. The doorman closed the door—and the light went on. We chugged off in our Chevy to spend the night in the humble cabin down the road, where we belonged.

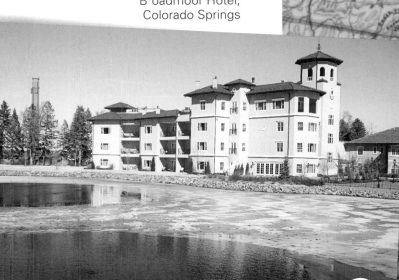

Broadmoor Hotel, Colorado Springs

granddaddy's beach house waited for me

By Curtis Carter, Augusta, Georgia

Granddaddy, Dr. King W. Milligan, had a clever way of letting me know I'd be included in our family's annual August sojourn to the beach. The first step of this ritual was my trip to Sapp's Barber Shop to get my annual "GI" haircut.

When that happened, I knew the aroma of salt spray and fish bait wasn't far off.

Before the dawn tinged the sky on that first day of August in Augusta, Georgia, Granddaddy was out in the backyard cinching down the tarpaulin on the trailer and checking the brake lights.

Next to Christmas, the day we left for the beach was, for me, one of the most exciting of the whole year.

My most vivid memory is the Cooper River Bridge. To me, it was a sight to behold.

Arching heavenward over Charleston Harbor, the huge narrow span was the last hurdle before

PEACHY TIMES AT THE BEACH. Summer fun awaited author when he and his grandfather (both pictured above) spent August at Isle of Palms, South Carolina. Hurricane Hugo destroyed their vacation house (top right) in 1989.

we pulled into our driveway at Vacationin', our family's beach retreat. Granddaddy was driving, his long-billed cap shading his eyes, his pipe clenched in his teeth and his hands keeping a steely grip on the steering wheel of the old Chevrolet as we began the crossing.

Over the Bridge

It was what I imagined a rollercoaster ride must be, all the way to the tickle in my stomach as we went up and down again and again.

Soon, we'd reach the end of the bridge and Granddaddy would laugh as if we had all just cheated death.

Minutes later, we were through Mount Pleasant and Sullivan's Island and crossing over the Breach Inlet Bridge. Soon I could jump into the cool waters of the Atlantic Ocean.

We were finally there—wild dunes and the ocean on the right and endless rows of slumbering beach houses on the left. Sitting there with its huge green shutters closed, Vacationin' almost looked asleep.

As we turned in the drive, though, I sensed the house was waking up from a long slumber.

After Granddaddy got out of the car, he just stood there, watching the house and murmuring to himself.

Today, as a grandfather myself, I know what he was thinking. His love for that house was as evident as his love for all of us. This house was his legacy to our family.

The house, one of so many along the South Carolina coast for nearly 100 years, had large bedrooms, high ceilings and a screened porch facing the ocean.

House Opening

I tagged along as Granddaddy fumbled with his keys and unlocked the front door. It swung open to a dark interior, and a musty, long-closed odor crinkled my nose. He cut on the electricity, and light flooded the rooms. One by one, the windows were raised and fresh sea air began washing away the odor of staleness.

The old-style kitchen had a wood-burning stove along with a modern electric range. Many a meal was prepared on that reliable woodstove when the island's electricity was knocked out by a thunderstorm.

The beach waited for us as we unloaded the trailer. The twilight was fast turning the ocean a deep shade of blue and the dunes a silvery gray.

Granddaddy and I trudged over the dunes for a few moments to look at the surf and then turned to look at the house. It was a moment of magic I'll always remember.

The sun setting behind the tin roof, the house all lit up, throwing off golden rays into growing dusk, Granddaddy holding my hand and Grandmother waving from the front stairs—no artist's painting could ever capture such a lovely moment.

BEACH PARTY. The scene on this California beach probably looks a bit different today than it did back in 1925. Dorothy Lane (the little girl at right, holding her doll) says that the Lanes had just moved to California from New Mexico and were gathered together with relatives for a picnic on the beach. Dorothy now lives in Albion, California.

DOIN' THE DUNES. While vacationing in Silver Lake, Michigan, Don, Jill and Dan Van Hoe had fun scrambling up and down the pristine sand dunes. The 1957 photo was taken by their father, Donald, of Kalamazoo, Michigan.

The Easiest Way to Travel with Children

If you're going away for a vacation, why not take the easiest way to travel with children!

As for cost, you can figure where you save. Air fares are surprisingly low. Drastic reductions have brought them down to an average of 4½¢ a mile.

As soon as your plans are set, make your reservations. Just phone the nearest Airline office or authorized Travel Agent. A majestic luxury airliner awaits at the gate. You step aboard with your wife and children. The stewardess greets you and makes you at home in your seats.

The plane takes off but you have no feeling of leaving the ground . . . no feeling of height or speed. Yet you're traveling along up to five miles a minute!

No wonder you're *there* almost before you know it . . . even before the children have a chance to get over their fascination at the scenes from their plane window. The children will love it.

P. S. In case your plans change, be sure to phone back and cancel your reservations. Air Transport Association of America, 1107 16th Street, N. W., Washington 6, D. C.

This advertisement is sponsored by the nation's airlines and leading manufacturers in the aviation industry

FLY THE PLANES THAT *FLY* THE U.S. FLAG
THE AIRLINES OF THE UNITED STATES

1946

fascinating niagara falls

NIAGARA FALLS FASHION. In the summer of 1932, Helen Ontai of Ewa Beach, Hawaii, and her family took a walking tour to the bottom of Niagara Falls. "To prevent getting drenched from the spray, we donned this rain gear," says Helen. "Not only was the attraction wet, the roar of the falling water was deafening. The trip was a once-in-a-lifetime thrill for me." The photo here shows (from left) dad Leonard, sisters Sophie and "Toots" and mother Adele. Young Helen is in the front.

There are no seven wonders of the world in the eyes of a child. There are seven million.

—WALT STREIGHTIFF

NATURAL WONDER. Family trips exposed kids to sights not found in their day-to-day world. While in Canada around 1956, the three children of Elinor Bernacki from Williamsville, New York, stood in awe of the beauty of Niagara Falls.

fun and folly of camping

CRY ME A RIVER.
"In 1953 daughter Cheryl was all set to go fishing with me, but her sister, Linda, preferred to stay back on shore!" recalls Bob Durling of Highland, Indiana.

CAMPING CUTIES.
"My family wasn't rich, but we always had fun," says Denise Hamilton of Springfield, Ohio. "Every August, we would go camping either in a tent or in the camper that Dad built. Grandpa, whom we called 'Pampaw,' would often join us with his boat." Here Denise (right) and her sister Peggy are vacationing on the Ohio River in 1959.

camping trip springs a leak

By Robert Spahr, Bradenton, Florida

I was so excited when Mom and Dad surprised me with a pup tent on my 13th birthday in June 1955! My dad helped me set it up in the yard for a campout that night, but I was eager to try it in the wild. My chance came that July when I traveled from home in Akron, Ohio, to visit my cousin and best friend, Eddie Martin, in Millersburg.

We told Eddie's mom we were going camping, but we weren't exactly sure where—probably a wooded lot on a nearby Amish farm. Aunt Ruthie was gone the afternoon Eddie and I packed up the tent with all the food we could find, and her best quilts. After hiking a few miles, we came across a neat little creek and decided to set up camp on a sandbar. Then we spent a glorious afternoon swimming, eating and having a great time. As the sun went down and the fire died out, we climbed into my tent, curled up under the quilts and settled down for the night.

When it started to rain, Eddie and I smiled at each other and peacefully fell back to sleep, feeling fortunate to be safe and sound inside a cozy tent. But around midnight, we were jolted awake—water was rushing through the bottom of the tent. By the time we escaped, the water was waist high and rising! In the pitch-black darkness, Eddie grabbed for our belongings, while I desperately hung onto my precious tent.

We headed to the edge of the creek and sat down to catch our breath. The creek kept rising, and lots of junk—including an old refrigerator—went floating past. After taking a quick inventory, Eddie and I realized we had lost our shoes, shirts, flashlights and even Aunt Ruthie's good quilts. I was happy to still have my tent in hand.

We scrambled up the steep bank, climbed over a barbed wire fence and hiked barefoot down a gravel road to the highway. Eventually, a good samaritan came to our aid. What a sight we must have been—two drenched 13-year-old boys lugging a waterlogged tent. I'm surprised he stopped!

When we arrived at Eddie's house, my aunt and uncle were waiting, along with the police, who had spent hours searching for us. Aunt Ruthie had planned a stern lecture but was so relieved that all she did was give us hugs—which lasted until she learned her quilts were lost during our adventure.

Yes, Eddie and I survived the worst flash flood in 50 years—and learned the hard way the importance of pitching a tent on higher ground!

MOTHER WAS KEEPER OF THE LIGHT

The one and only camping trip our family took was in 1932, when I was 9. We camped in the Adirondack Mountains near Speculator, New York, about 100 miles from home.

The first night was anything but restful, as we slept in a tent with only a blanket and a few newspapers between us and the hard, lumpy ground.

Then, because my mother was afraid a wild animal would get us, she snapped on the flashlight at the least little sound. None of us got very much shut-eye.

The second night was better, as we stayed in a rented cottage with friends. There had been rumors of break-ins near the area, so I hid my good shoes in the cottage before we went to a nearby lake the next morning.

At the end of the trip, we were halfway back home to Morrisville, New York, when I remembered my shoes were still under the sofa where I'd hidden them.

—*Esther Davis, Live Oak, Florida*

SIX KIDS TOPPED HIS LIMIT

In 1946, my dad belatedly married his high school sweetheart. He had three kids and so did she. There were plenty of adjustments to be made and plenty of adventures on our new family's first camping trip.

It was in the summer of 1947, at Wattum Lake near Mount Hood, Oregon. I got too far out in the lake, stepped in a deep hole and went under. I didn't know how to swim, but my new big brother dove in and rescued me.

Then my new sister Marge was "helping" when the kerosene stove in the tent exploded and covered everything, including Marge, with soot.

That was the last straw for my dad, who was normally patient. "Taking all six children camping at one time is too much trouble," he declared. "I will never do it again!"

And he didn't.

—*Donna Wilson Armstrong*
Gig Harbor, Washington

Growing Up

1950

their first camping trip was almost their last

A BAD TRIP AT THE START TURNED INTO A MEMORABLE TIME.

We borrowed just about everything, including Grandpa's 1947 Chevrolet, for our first camping holiday in July 1955. Dad, an engineer, had made a cartop carrier for the tent and other equipment.

We didn't have air mattresses or sleeping bags, so we packed blankets. For our first night's meal, Mom made a batch of chili, which she stored on the shelf behind the backseat.

Our destination was Algonquin Provincial Park in northern Ontario, a trip that would take most of the day from our home in Kitchener, according to Dad.

For a while, we four children in the backseat amused ourselves with road games. But as the day wore on, our spirits wore down. When it started to rain, we just wanted Dad to turn the car around and go home.

The rain became torrential and Dad had to slow the car to a crawl. The heavy downpour made us miss a sign announcing a motorcycle race, and soon motorcycles were coming at us like bullets.

At one point, Dad had to cut across the road to avoid a collision. When the car came to a jolting stop, our faces were pressed against the windows as we watched our cartop carrier fly into a hay field.

OH DEER, WHAT A TRIP. The Krause family was ready to roll in 1955 (opposite); author is second from left. In photo above right, she has her hand out to a deer. Mom Carla and the kids posed at Algonquin Provincial Park during their 1955 camping trip (above). The kids are, from left, Pam, Christine, Rick and Penny. At right, Pam, Penny and Christine are playing with walking sticks.

Having been in the military, Dad was prepared and had packed his fisherman's rubber raincoat. After he repositioned and repacked the cartop carrier, we were on our way.

The rain stopped and the sun came out. When we finally arrived at the park, we were tired and starving, so Mom brought out the chili and we all dug in.

Dad put up the tent, which was made of musty-smelling oilcloth. The tent had no floor, so Dad used canvas tarps and old army groundsheets.

The rain returned that night. I awoke to the sounds of the drops thudding on the tent and of Dad digging a trench around the perimeter with his trusty army shovel.

But the rain was already coming through the holes in the tent. My face and hair were wet, and even worse, my stomach hurt.

The chili, which had sat in the sun on the car's rear seat shelf, showed no mercy. I left the tent and joined the rest of the family searching for the latrine that Dad said he'd dug about 100 yards away.

Above the drone of the pelting rain and claps of thunder, I heard Dad tell Mom we were packing up in the morning and going home.

But the next morning the sun came out, and Mom and Dad decided to try to dry things out as best they could before packing.

In the meantime, we explored the park by car, stopping from time to time to have our hands nuzzled by moist, soft noses of the deer that ventured out to the side of the road.

As it turned out, that extra day turned into two weeks of fun.

Over the years, Mom and Dad became "professionals" at camping, and we kids loved it.

—*Christine Krause Schiestel*
Port Elgin, Ontario

Road Trip!

dad made scouting outing special

By Don Whyte, Birchwood, Wisconsin

In 1934, my dad, R.B. Whyte, invited Boy Scout Troop 22 to spend the weekend at our cabin on Paddock Lake, west of our home in Kenosha, Wisconsin.

I don't recall how all of us traveled the 17 miles to the lake, but I know at times there were a dozen or more kids in Dad's seven-passenger 1929 Nash.

In the photo above, Dad is in the dark sweater, I'm the kid with no shirt just left of the tree and my brother, Dode, is at the left side of the table with his chin in his hand. Our scoutmaster, Leo Konrad, is standing third from left.

There was only a small kerosene stove in the cabin, so the cooking was done outside on the stone fireplace. The copper boiler on top was used to make Dad's favorite meal for the gang—layers of corn on the cob, potatoes, wieners and sauerkraut, all covered with water.

You'll notice the only boy with any part of a Boy Scout uniform was Ray Kaufman on the far right. Few of us could afford uniforms, and those who could didn't wear them for fear of ruining them during our games of hide-and-seek and Annie over.

There were some great campfire stories, and at night, even though there were lots of beds in the cabin, several of us boys spent the night on the porch floor.

the day the circus came to town

As the fourth child of five during the Depression, any kind of outing was a rare occasion. So in the summer of 1939, my heart fluttered with pride knowing I was the only one in the family willing to arise early to accompany Daddy to watch the circus train arrive.

Hand in hand, we walked the streets and alleyways, reaching the train in time to hear the low whistle announcing its arrival. The huge hooves of horses thumped in unison as they dragged the cars off the track. I could almost reach out and touch the circus wagons that had been beautifully carved to tell the stories of favorite nursery rhymes, like the old woman who lived in a shoe. With trunks swinging, huge elephants were guided by haggard men. I was speechless and couldn't wait to tell my friends! As if by magic, a huge tent arose, blocking out the rising sun. It was a wonderful sight.

It didn't matter to me that we couldn't afford to attend the circus acts. I had just spent a priceless morning with my father. All these years later, I still feel the joy of that memorable day!

—*Dolores Slane, New Berlin, Wisconsin*

FARM VISITS THRILLED CITY KIDS

It took 14 hours on narrow dirt roads to get to Grandmother's farm, but the two weeks my brother and I spent there each summer flew by!

Every day after milking, we would take the cows to a pasture about a mile away. After they were settled, my brother and I would fill our pails with wild berries so Grandmother could bake a pie for that evening's dessert. We'd while away the hours jumping in the hay and playing in the outhouse, which Grandmother had decorated with curtains and a little vase of flowers.

Our days on the farm were such happy times for us city kids, and we often didn't want to leave when Mom and Dad arrived. But memories of Grandmother traveled with us on our journey home in the form of her tender fried chicken and homemade bread.

—*Adeline Ellison, Modesto, California*

long trail led to lasting memories

Every summer in the 1930s, my family eagerly traveled to the tiny hamlet of Jacksonville, Vermont, to visit my grandparents on the farm where Dad grew up. For my sister and me, the highlight of the vacation was the annual three- to four-day hike with Dad on the Long Trail, a 270-mile spur of the Appalachian Trail.

On the appointed morning, we loaded the car with our properly packed knapsacks, and Mom would drop us off at the trailhead. While she headed back to the farm for a few days of peace and quiet, Dad, my sister and I began our adventure.

The huts built and maintained by the local Long Trail clubs varied considerably in their comforts. It was as much fun staying in the rustic, three-sided open shelters as it was in the rare fully enclosed cabins. You never knew who would share your space. On one unforgettable trek, we met a happy-go-lucky hiker who happened to be my mom's cousin, Malcolm. While our meals were carefully planned to require the fewest ingredients possible, Malcolm carried fresh eggs and treated us to an elegant camp breakfast one morning. Pancakes never tasted so good!

Tired as we were from hiking each day, our sleep was never very deep. The blanket rolls we toted kept us warm but didn't cushion the hard plank bunks. And the spruce branches we cut as aromatic mattresses didn't provide much relief.

We always signed the log at each stop and scanned the previous entries. Occasionally there would be an "end-to-ender"—someone who had started far south in Georgia and was traveling the whole Appalachian Trail up to Mount Katahdin in Maine. My mind boggled at the logistics of hiking for months, replenishing supplies en route and keeping up a regular pace regardless of fatigue. Even on our limited excursions, we kids grew weary.

Hiking through the thick woods, the air was close and we had to battle clouds of mosquitoes. But what a difference when the trees thinned out and the vistas expanded. The stunning view from the peak—enhanced by our struggle to get there—made it all worthwhile.

During the final hours of our expedition, I'd find myself lagging, only to sprint ahead again. With mixed emotions, we would eventually spy Mom waiting for us at the arranged time and place. I hated to leave behind that special feeling of accomplishment—but, oh, how I welcomed the hot bath and comfy bed at Grandma's!

—*Dorothy Conlon, Sarasota, Florida*

PARROT JUNGLE
MIAMI, FLORIDA

birds of a feather

We took our kids (from left) Billy, Bruce, Susan and Linda to Miami's Jungle Island in 1968. Although a bird isn't perched on Bruce's left arm, he was sure to strike a pose like his older siblings.

—*Odette Landers, Fort Pierce, Florida*

CHAPTER THREE

Rites of Passage

Losing baby teeth, shaving, learning a skill, dating, first jobs…childhood is filled with memorable moments that take kids one step closer to becoming adults. Sometimes we felt we really were maturing—and other times we didn't.

"When I turned 10 in 1918, my dad and Uncle Izzy invited me to join them on their Saturday morning trips to a Turkish bath in Brooklyn, New York. I was thrilled!" shares Murray Shaw of Phoenix, Arizona. "Having never learned to swim, I found the swimming pool to be especially intriguing. So that I could safely swim without fear of drowning, Uncle Izzy bought me water wings, which were two cork-filled bags that attached to the waist with strings.

"But I longed to be like the other men, who simply dove in. I decided to place the water wings on the surface and jump on top of them. With my inexperience, I didn't anticipate that the water wings would move from the weight of my body. The strings caught onto my toes, causing my head to go down into the water.

"I tried to shake my legs free, but the strings were tangled. I thought surely I'd drown. Just as I was about to give up, I was pulled out of the water. After much choking and coughing, I looked up to see Uncle Izzy's anxiety-filled face. He had saved my life—and reminded me I was not yet a man."

Read on for more unforgettable firsts that shaped our childhoods....

his first shave drew a crowd

By Rose Ramsay, Ashland, Oregon

My big brother, Dean, was 14 years old and had skin as smooth as a baby's. So one day when he asked Dad about shaving, it created a stir.

Dad was deeply engrossed in reading the *Chronicle* at the time.

"Dad, can I borrow your razor?" asked Dean. When there was no response, Dean repeated the question a little louder.

Dad lowered the newspaper to peer at Dean over the top. "What for?"

There was a brief silence. Then Dean squared his shoulders and took a deep breath. "To…uh…shave."

"Really?" Dad pushed his glasses up the bridge of his nose, laid the paper aside and surveyed Dean with interest. Meanwhile, Grandma, who was sitting beside Dad on the couch, almost jabbed herself with her darning needle.

"You don't need to shave!" Grandma said. She turned to Dad and exclaimed, "Look at those cheeks—that boy could star in a cold cream commercial!"

"Aw, Grandma," protested Dean.

Mother stepped from the kitchen with a tea towel in her hand. "You're too young to shave," she told Dean.

Dad scowled. "Come here, son," he said. He carefully examined Dean's jawline through his bifocals.

Whiskerless Wonder

"Well?" Dean sounded anxious. I came over for a look and didn't see one whisker—although I was too kind to say so.

Finally, Dad nodded his consent. Dean happily marched off to the bathroom with me at his heels.

"Be sure not to dull my razor," Dad called after him.

"You be careful," came Mother's voice from the kitchen.

"You'll ruin your skin," warned Grandma.

Dad's shaving tools were above the sink. Dean ran some hot water into the basin, splashed a little on his face and pumped a mound of shaving foam into his palm. He began spreading it on.

"That's an awful lot of shaving cream,"

NICE AND SMOOTH. Dean Ramsay's whiskerless cheeks were the product of his first shave—whether he needed it or not. Dean earned a battle scar that day, a telltale nick on the chin.

CHILDREN: J.C. ALLEN AND SON

lost tooth brought lots of loot

At 5, I was the youngest child around when Uncle Richard, Aunt Sally and their teenage children came to visit my family one summer in Berthoud, Colorado. One night during their stay, I lost my first tooth! I had imagined all sorts of ways it might happen the first time—perhaps by chewing on some candy (my idea) or tying it with string to a doorknob (my brother's idea). But it turned out to be uneventful: The tooth simply fell out on its own. I headed up to bed, safely tucking the tiny thing under my pillow before turning in for the night.

Little did I know that everyone else in the house was afraid my parents would forget the occasion amid the excitement of having guests. So they all decided to take matters into their own hands to save me from disappointment.

First, my parents sneaked in to deposit the usual quarter. Rewarding me with some of their hard-earned money, my four teenage siblings were next, followed by my cousins. After Aunt Sally left several dollars, Uncle Richard took a turn.

You can imagine my delight the next morning when I lifted my pillow to discover that the tooth fairy had left me a small fortune. Uncle Richard alone gave me a whole $20! I scooped up the cash and ran downstairs to tell everyone the exciting news. They were all speechless, but this thrilled girl barely noticed. When I went back upstairs to count my loot and deposit it in my piggy bank, I heard a roar of laughter coming from the kitchen.

To this day, I wonder how so many people sneaked into my room without waking me—and without running into each other in the hallway!

—*Laura Piedad, Greensboro, North Carolina*

Rites of Passage

hysterical hairy moments

Whether done by a professional barber or by an unruly sibling, early haircuts were likely most traumatic for Mom!

IF DAD CAN DO IT...

"In 1957, my husband, Robert, took our son, Dean, for his first-ever haircut (left), in Reading, Pennsylvania, and he proved to be a very good boy indeed," says Marion Yeager from Temple. "Robert got his hair trimmed the same day, so I think that's why Dean was so well behaved."

haircut derailed

My brothers, John and Bill, ages 8½ and 6, had just returned from the barbershop in our town of Kingston, West Virginia, when they asked me if I'd like a haircut. Being a curious 4-year-old, I said, "OK."

They piled catalogs on a kitchen chair for me to sit on and draped Mom's tablecloth around my shoulders.

Next, Bill took his windup Lionel train engine and, with the wheels spinning, went up the side of my head. My hair wound around all eight wheels so tightly that the locomotive was stuck there—with the whistle blowing! My ears rang for a week.

Mom came running, and it seemed like it took hours to get the train wheels cut away from my head. All of my long hair went with it. As you can see from the photo (right), my mom used a hair bow to cover my bald spot.

—*Betty Stephenson, Dover, Delaware*

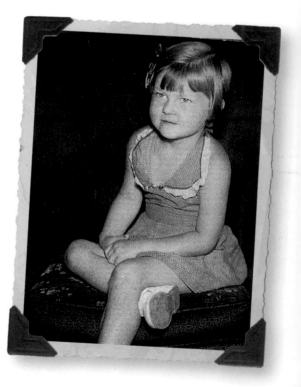

Growing Up

MISCHIEVOUS MOMENT.
"In the photo at left, you can see that my brother, Andrew, was blessed with a cute curl on the top of his head when he was 18 months old," says Louise Collier of Redding, California. "I must have been jealous, because one day I told sweet, trusting Andrew to sit very still and then proceeded to cut that curl right off. Luckily, my scandalous act didn't stop Andrew and me from becoming the best of chums through the years."

haircut made perfect snipshot

"My son, George Voyzey, was about 10 months old when he got his first haircut, in November 1959," writes George Voyzey Jr. of Phillipsburg, Pennsylvania.

"The barber was my uncle, Ray Croyle, and the haircut occurred in the kitchen of my parents, George and Delma Voyzey, in Chester Hill, near Phillipsburg."

ALMOST FINISHED. George clings to his mother (above) as Uncle Ray takes a little off the top, but is in a better mood after a bath (right).

events were elementary and exciting

SCHOOL DAYS MADE GRADE-A MEMORIES.

OFF TO SCHOOL. "It was the first day of school in 1920 for me (in the hair ribbon) and my brother, Raymond," remembers Marjorie Leborgne of Laguna Hills, California. "Raymond was 5 and was going into first grade because there was no kindergarten in Kingston, New York, where we lived. I was 7 and starting third grade. Our sister, Alma, was 3 and too young for school. She stayed home with our mother, who is behind us."

three cheers for boppie!

By Richard Dake, Largo, Florida

An eighth-grade graduation may not be a milestone for everyone. But thanks to my grandfather, I still vividly recall mine from 1946.

The preparations were intense. Our sour-faced, disagreeable principal—I'll call her "Miss X"—spent hours explaining the rules to us. We must wear the appropriate clothing under our blue robes. We were to sit up straight, be quiet and not fidget during the speeches. When our names were called, we should rise, receive our diploma, shake her hand, walk back to our seat and sit down.

But her biggest concern was the applause.

There was to be none—absolutely none—until after the last student had his or her diploma clutched firmly in hand and was once again seated. Over and over again she mentioned this. No applause until the end of the ceremony. We all went home and warned our families about Miss X's adamant views on applauding.

The big night arrived. My hair was combed, with the curl restrained. My tie was straight. My shirt and pants were pressed. On went the blue robe and hat with the tassel topping all that glory. We marched in alphabetical order onto the stage to sit on the uncomfortable wooden folding

COMMENCEMENT DRESS. "Formal gowns and roses were a graduation tradition in Chamblee, Georgia," writes Vickie Bettis Strickland. "I was able to buy the dress and flowers with a $25 war bond my mother had bought in 1946 and given to my aunt to hold for me before she passed away when I was 12." In this 1952 photo, Vickie is fourth from the right.

chairs. The speeches began. The speeches continued. The speeches were over. Finally, the first student's name was called. The next 13 names were called, and then it was my turn.

I stood up and walked to Miss X to receive my diploma. As I turned to go back to my seat, two hands loudly clapped in the hallowed silence of the auditorium. Gasp! My grandfather! Silence. I kept walking. Again, the two hands clapped. The rhythm slowly picked up momentum. More and more hands joined in, until everyone in the audience was energetically applauding.

Seething with anger, Miss X instructed me to sit down. I sat, but the applause grew louder. She shouted, "Stand up!" I stood up. The

laughter and applause of more than 500 people in the audience became deafening.

To our principal's dismay, my class joined in the uproar. Miss X shouted several more times for me to sit down and stand up, only to have more clapping and cheering follow.

Looking as if she would burst every blood vessel in her head, Miss X grabbed the microphone and shouted, "Evidently, Richard, someone else was as surprised that you graduated as I was!" The applause and laughter went on for several more minutes before the ceremony resumed and continued without incident.

My "Boppie," God bless him, had made my eighth-grade graduation something to remember.

tv heroes inspired her to be brave

The summer of 1954 was over, and the first day of school had finally arrived. I may have been only 5 years old, but I was ready. After all, I had been to school once with my aunt Sue on her last day of sixth grade. But most important, I had my brand-spanking-new Roy Rogers and Dale Evans lunch box. I was all prepared!

Instead of putting me on the big yellow bus on that special first day, my mother asked my dad to drive me to Glenville Elementary, which sat atop a very high hill. I'm sure she assumed he would not only drive me but walk me to my class. But Dad had another idea. He drove me to the bottom of the hill, wished me well and went on his way.

I felt so small when I gazed at all the steps going up the hill. With my trusty lunch box heroes at my side, I took a deep breath and began the trek, my short legs climbing the steep steps along the meandering sidewalk. Finally, I reached the top to find the biggest sea of children I had ever seen. Where was I to go? I asked a tall, smart-looking boy, who only chuckled unkindly.

My feelings were hurt and a tear ran down my cheek, but I regained my composure. If the real Roy Rogers had been close by, I knew he'd tell me to be brave. Trailing behind kids who appeared to be my size, I walked with head held high into the school and found Mrs. Rohrbaugh's first-grade classroom.

That was a day of many firsts for me—my first day of school, my first lunch box (which I still have!) and my first adventure out in the big world all alone.

—*Wanda Harrell, Kingsland, Georgia*

DIPLOMA, SEE? "My son Kent posed with his certificate after graduating in May 1962 from Ludwigsburg American Nursery School, which was actually located in Pattonville, Germany," relates Howard Headley from Sherman, Texas. It looks as if the teacher needed to check the spelling of Kent's last name.

primary performances

Recitals and plays are the first big events when kids face the public. Although that public is mostly family and friends, it's an experience never forgotten.

DRESSED FOR DANCE.
"Daughters Kathleen and Marianne—8 and 10 years old, respectively—were dressed as glowworms for a dance recital when this photo was taken in 1963," explains Ruth Polchek, King of Prussia, Pennsylvania. "They took lessons for years in Philadelphia and really thought they were on their way to becoming prima ballerinas!"

FLASHY PHOTO.
"I don't remember much about this Tom Thumb wedding at St. Mark Evangelical Lutheran Church in Brookline, Pennsylvania, other than this picture being taken in 1925," confesses Dorothy Dedlow of DeLand, Florida. "To this day, I can still remember how startled I was when the flash went off with a bang and a puff of smoke. I was the groom's mother, standing behind his left shoulder."

first jobs were priceless

EARNING MONEY WAS EMPOWERING FOR KIDS.

helping uncle sam

"This photo of my older brother, Don, was taken in 1942 by *The Des Moines Register* and *Des Moines Tribune* newspapers to publicize the war effort contributed by newspaper carriers," says Gene Chiodo of Effingham, Illinois. "At age 15, Don was also the branch manager for newspaper delivery. He and I both carried morning and evening papers, and we knew customers were eager to get the latest war news." Marcy Merrill of North Cove, Washington, brought color to this great World War II-era picture for us.

the disney connection

During the Great Depression, I worked at the Uptown Theater in Marceline, Missouri. I started at age 12 delivering handbills, eventually became head usher and finally was the one who opened and closed the theater. For six or seven years, I saw every movie that came to town.

Marceline is the boyhood home of Walt Disney. In fact, Main Street at Disneyland is designed to resemble Main Street in Marceline, right down to the Uptown Theater.

Walt and his brother, Roy, often visited Marceline. In the '50s, one of Walt's movies had its world premiere there and ran nonstop for 24 hours so everyone in town could see it.

It was great to have worked in a theater that became famous. I still think the old movies were the best ever made.

—*Dude Boddy, Pasco, Washington*

> *There is always one moment in childhood when the door opens and lets the future in.*
>
> —GRAHAM GREENE

it pays to be nice

The summer of 1943, when I was 16, my mother said that if I wanted nice things, I should earn the money to pay for them.

I got a job at the soda fountain at Quartetti's drugstore in Chicago's Grand and Harlem shopping area. I worked hard for my 25 cents an hour, coming in early and staying late.

I learned to keep a smile on my face and to treat people the way I'd want to be treated.

After a few months, I was promoted to cashier at the cigar and cigarette counter, then later became clerk for the whole store. Eventually I became the store's cosmetics buyer.

I stayed there after I was married in 1947 and worked until 1950, when I had my first baby. That job was a great way to learn how to treat the public.

—*Martha Evans Kruse*
Round Rock, Texas

A FEW FLOWERS...is what the perfume sign says in French in this 1940s photograph of Martha Evans Kruse. She started in the drugstore at age 16 and worked her way up.

no one forgets their first car!

A drive for independence led to motoring memories.

sweet 16 surprise

Daddy promised to take me to the county seat so I could apply for my driver's license when I turned 16 on March 10, 1946.

On the big day, I jumped out of bed but was disappointed when he said we had to take his car into town for repairs.

This was not the way I wanted to spend my 16th birthday, but as always, I did as I was told.

When we arrived at Lank Phoebus Auto, Daddy pulled around back, then got out and motioned for me to follow him in. Once inside the shop, I heard Lank, the owner, call for me to come up front to the showroom.

There, all alone, was a brand-new 1946 maroon Dodge convertible wrapped with a large ribbon and tied with a huge bow. Taped to the windshield was a big card that read, "Happy Birthday from Mother and Daddy." I let out a scream and even cried.

Since there was actually nothing wrong with Daddy's car, I got to drive mine right off the showroom floor. I put down the top even though it was cold outside.

I got my driver's license that day and later picked up some friends. We tooled around with the top down and the radio turned up.

Back then, gasoline was 16 cents a gallon. Daddy told the service station owner where he bought his gas to let me charge mine. The first month, I charged $20 worth!

I kept the Dodge (in photo above) for three years, until I married and needed something more practical. I've had many more cars since, but none has meant as much as my first.

—*Peggy Tull, Crisfield, Maryland*

SAVED BY A BOOT LACE.

When I was a high school senior, my pride and joy was my 1936 Ford. That's me with the car in the photo taken in 1942.

One winter evening it was snowing hard, and I had a nine-mile drive from town to home. The vacuum-powered windshield wiper couldn't handle the wet, heavy snow.

I tried driving with my head out the window, but that was even worse. Then I got an idea.

I took the laces out of my boots and tied them together. Then I tied one end of the laces to the wiper and ran the other end back into the car, through the wing windows and back to the wiper, where I tied it.

Driving with one hand and pulling the boot laces back and forth, I made it home just fine.

—*Bob Marcum, Silverton, Oregon*

he earned car the old-fashioned way

By Donald Braverman, Jacksonville, Florida

In the summer of 1954, my 17th birthday was approaching and I could hardly wait to buy a car. When I spotted a 1930 Model A Ford for sale in the Esso station parking lot, I just had to stop and ask the owner, Mr. Murphy, how much he wanted for it. The answer was $25. I rushed home.

When I told Dad about the car, he said he thought a Model A was very dependable and that I should go ahead and get it.

"Thanks, Dad, but I don't have the $25 right now," I replied. "Will you lend it to me?"

My dad looked at me and said, "If you really want that car, you're bound to find 50 people who need their lawns cut."

I was crushed. I earned only 50 cents for each lawn. And we had a push mower, which meant I had to rake the clippings and use a pair of scissors to do the trimming. But my dad made an arrangement with Mr. Murphy to hold the car for me and to take payments in installments.

I spent the summer behind that lawn mower.

Each week, I'd give Mr. Murphy all the money I had earned. Finally, the magic day came. I felt like a king as I drove the black beauty home for a good washing and waxing.

When Dad got home from work, he told me to hop in and start it up. Dad listened for a moment before saying, "Quick! Shut it off!"

I panicked as Dad asked me to go get his toolbox. When I returned, he rolled up his sleeves, popped the hood, tinkered with a wrench and then came out from under the hood with the distributor cap in hand.

"Now, young man," he said, "you can have this back after you buy insurance."

With insurance costing $85, it took five more months of lawn work, shoveling snow and other odd jobs before I could drive my car.

Sure, I was disappointed. But as time went on, I grew to respect Dad. He taught me the importance of working toward a goal—and of being the kind of dad who passed that valuable lesson on to my own kids.

puppy love

FROM CRUSHES TO DATING, WE WORE OUR HEARTS ON OUR SLEEVES.

ARE THEY HERE YET? "Our son, Rand, 14, and daughter, Rhonda, 16, were all dressed up and waiting for their dates to pick them up for a school dance in 1968," says Betty Berney of Phillipsburg, Kansas. "It was Rand's first date, and he was a bit anxious and looking out the window to see if the dates were coming. This was at our home in Phillipsburg."

DOWN TO EARTH. "Steve was a football and basketball player, and I was a cheerleader," says Dorothy Schernick, New London, Wisconsin "He asked me out for the first time in 1955 while I was handing out programs for a pep rally. Our song was, and still is, *Earth Angel.*"

PLAID PALS. "The reason for our formal dress was the 1956 senior prom at the Needham, Massachusetts, high school," writes Richard Crisafulli (on left) of Algood, Tennessee. "The photo, taken by my father, shows me and one of my best friends, Mark Eaton, and our dates, Carol Dunbar and Carolyn. I can't remember Carolyn's last name because she didn't go to our high school. The picture was taken just before we left for the prom. If you look closely, you can see that the cummerbunds Mark and I are wearing match our plaid bow ties. That was quite novel at the time."

first crush took the cake

By Milt Neuhauser, Phillips, Wisconsin

The year 1931 marked the start of my first crush. It began when the wife of the local undertaker, who was newly arrived in Flanagan, Illinois, ordered two birthday cakes from my stepmother, the best baker in town.

On the Saturday morning of the birthday party, my sister, Helen, and I delivered the cakes to the Carrigan home.

My knock on the back door of the house was answered by a very attractive tall lady.

"We are delivering the birthday cakes you ordered, ma'am," Helen said.

"Well, now," Mrs. Carrigan said, "bring them in and we'll see what you have."

Gingerly, we carried the large cardboard box into the kitchen and placed it on the table.

Mrs. Carrigan removed the tan butcher paper covering the box and exclaimed, "Oh, they look just perfect for Margaret's party this afternoon!"

"And who is this cute fella?" Mrs. Carrigan said, rumpling my already messed-up hair.

"This is my baby brother," Helen said. "He's 9, too, so he must be in your daughter's class."

"Then, in that case, we must invite him to our party this afternoon," Mrs. Carrigan said. "Would you like that, young man?"

"I guess so," I stammered.

Back home, my stepmother was reluctant. "Your clothes just aren't nice enough for those folks," she said.

But Helen finally convinced her. "He'd better go," she said, "or Mrs. Carrigan may not order more baked goods."

My sisters helped me get dressed in the only good clothes I had—knickers, black stockings and a too-small blue shirt.

The party turned out to be great! There

I was excited, scared and nervous just thinking about it. I'd never gone to a birthday party—never even had one of my own, for that matter.

were treats and lawn games, including croquet, which I was pretty good at.

When the birthday cakes were cut, we were each given a choice, plus a huge scoop of smooth store-bought ice cream.

Margaret was dressed up real pretty in a white dress, with white shoes and a pink ribbon in her beautiful black hair. When she opened her gifts, I felt foolish. I'd brought only a small homemade card.

But when the party was over and I was leaving, Margaret ran up to me, gave me a big kiss on the cheek and said, "Thanks for coming to my party. Your mother's cakes were real good. See you in school."

I didn't know what to say. I'd never been kissed before, except by my sisters.

I was really smitten and couldn't believe the prettiest girl in school kissed me!

From then on, my studies suffered. All I could do was stare at this new girl and think, *This is the prettiest girl I've ever seen.*

Now and then, she would let me walk her home and carry her books and her fancy pencil box. Most of the time, I was tongue-tied and didn't know what to say.

My bubble burst the next summer, though. The girl of my dreams moved and I never heard from her again.

digging into the facts of life

By Evelyn Rhodes Smith, Charleston, West Virginia

Growing up on a farm, I had the chore of letting our Jersey cows out before the sun rose each morning. One day, as I approached the stall of my favorite cow, Bessie, I noticed unusual movement. At her side was a newborn calf nursing. Greatly excited, I ran back to the house to wake everyone with the wonderful news.

I was shocked when no one was surprised. After breakfast, Grandma came with me to the barn. As a 5-year-old, I thought Grandma was the smartest person in the world. After all, she had a ready answer for each one of my questions. So I asked her where the little calf had come from, when it wasn't there the night before.

Quietly, Grandma replied, "Bessie dug it out of a bank."

As I mulled this over, it made sense to me. Dad turned up mice when he plowed the fields. I'd seen an opossum come out of the bank near our spring with babies hugging her back.

> *Soon, with my shovel and little metal bucket in hand, I began to dig holes all over the yard, looking for babies I could free.*

When I asked if I, too, had come from the ground, she assured me I had. I promised Grandma not to tell a soul about my newfound knowledge.

A short time afterward, I heard Mom say Aunt Effie had to rest in bed for two weeks after the birth of her baby. I knew it was because she had hurt herself digging the baby out of the ground.

Soon, with my shovel and little metal bucket in hand, I began to dig holes all over the yard, looking for babies I could free.

Mom asked what I was up to, but I couldn't divulge the secret Grandma and I shared. Eventually, all the small mounds of dirt around the yard had my mother at her wits' end, and she demanded an answer. That was the day I retired my shovel and learned the truth about the birds and the bees!

Many years later, someone asked my husband and me why we didn't have children. Ted jokingly replied, "I hid her shovel."

first time fishing was reel-y fun!

gone fishin'

"My uncle, George Mowbray, was an avid amateur photographer who captured me fishing for the first time on a river near my grandparents' house," recalls Mike Mowbray of Fond du Lac, Wisconsin. "I enjoy fishing to this day, given the success of my first experience when I was 5!"

WHAT A MESS!

"Our son Rich, then 5, had just returned from his first fishing trip with his grandfather Howard Jones," writes Bill Young of Oneida, New York. "The slide was taken in August 1962 at our house in Oneida." There are a couple of nice perch showing in that mess of fish Rich is displaying.

learning to skate
gave her a scare

Times were tough in the late 1930s, so my grandmother opened her home to Aunt Louise, Uncle Carroll, five unmarried aunts, my mom, my dad and me. As the only child, I had relatives as my playmates, rescuing me from what could have been a lonely girlhood.

A favorite memory is of Aunt Louise giving me an early present for my fifth birthday—a brand-new pair of roller skates. They had wide brown leather bands that laced across the toes and no ball bearings in the wheels. My aunt assured me the wheels wouldn't go too fast, but when I spun them around with my finger they seemed awfully speedy to me.

After I put on the skates, Aunt Louise held my hand and walked beside me as I tried to get the feel of them. I promptly slipped from her grasp, skinned my knees, took off the skates, plopped into a lawn chair and refused to budge, tears streaming down my cheeks.

Aunt Louise quickly ran into the house and came out with her own skates. I watched her maneuver gracefully up and down the narrow sidewalk—even skating backward!—as she hummed the *Skater's Waltz*.

Soon she glided back to me, put the skates back on my feet and pried my hands loose from the chair. My ankles wobbled, but Aunt Louise kept saying, "You can do it. Just slide and glide. Slide and glide."

Skating backward, my aunt held tightly to my hands and helped me with small movements. Finally I got the hang of it. My mom and other aunts came outside to cheer me on. Before long, I was skating on my own. I'll always remember how Aunt Louise lovingly taught me never to give up when faced with a challenge.

—*Carolyn Mingus, Evergreen, Colorado*

© H. ARMSTRONG ROBERTS / CORBIS

parents sacrificed for sacrament

Although the country was not far from entering World War II on May 4, 1941, it was the last thing on my mind when I awoke that day. I was preoccupied with a more personal matter. After three years of studying, I was about to make my first Holy Communion.

Like so many families at the time, we were poor. Our parents scrimped to provide their children with a place to live and food to eat. I can only imagine how they sacrificed to dress their young ones for this special event. These were not outfits to be worn every day, but parents believed in the importance of being properly dressed and photographed to document the occasion. A magnificent, memorable Sunday it was.

—*Dick Washburn, Cumberland, North Carolina*

Fabulous Fashions

Knickers...feed-sack dresses...corkscrew curls...poodle skirts. Our first encounters with fashion take place in our youth. Every generation has fallen victim to a fad that we either remember fondly or dread to this day.

"My mother and aunt made me a crepe-paper concoction for our little Minnesota town's annual parade around 1933," recalls Delores Gustafson of Colorado Springs, Colorado.

"I hated that dress and refused to wear it. It rustled when I walked, and I couldn't sit down without ruining the flower in back that matched the one in the front.

"But my mother and aunt were persistent and convinced me that the parade would be a short one, so I reluctantly agreed to wear it. I think the expression on my face in the photo at right shows my frustration with that dress!"

Turn the page and take a look at some of the fashions and hairstyles that have come and gone through the years.

flowered feed sacks made me tough

By Richard Paugh, Columbus, Ohio

Life was difficult during the Great Depression, and it got even tougher after my brother and I were forced to wear shirts made of floral-print feed sacks.

I was born in 1925, and Father was a partner in a Studebaker dealership in Akron, Ohio, before the Depression hit. Eventually, with only one car on the sales floor at a time, the agency went broke and hard times found our family.

We lost our home and moved into various rental houses but still found ways to live full, healthy lives.

When we could, we lived off the land, picking wild berries and growing beans, peppers, corn and tomatoes.

Every spring, we'd buy 100 baby chicks to raise and later sell. It was my job to feed the flock, clean the henhouse and gather the eggs. If a neighbor wanted a chicken, I had to kill and clean the bird—all this before I was 10 years old.

My standard "uniform" included tennis shoes with the big toes worn out. This was OK in warmer months, but when winter hit northern Ohio, I'd cover the holes with the cardboard dividers from a box of Shredded Wheat cereal.

Somewhere along the line, Mom got a pattern for boys' shirts. Her main source for fabric was the floral-patterned sacks that the chicken feed came in.

Mom would labor away on her treadle sewing machine until my brother, Bill, and I had new shirts. I know she tried hard to find feed sacks that had a "masculine" print, but I'm afraid the finished product never looked too manly. At school, the other boys made life rough on us, making cracks about our flowered "girls' shirts."

I spent many a recess taking on our detractors. Sometimes I won, sometimes I lost. Most times I got my shirt torn up and faced another battle at home explaining.

POST-FEED SACK. Richard Paugh (at right in front) and brother Bill sported their first store-bought shirts for a photograph with their mom and dad, Agnes and Bryan.

"Along the way, I learned how to take life as it came, no matter how the dice played out."   —RICHARD PAUGH

Along the way, I learned how to take life as it came, no matter how the dice played out.

Later, my family moved to Columbus, and life got better. For one thing, I actually got to wear store-bought clothes. But my early years of wearing flowered shirts had helped season me for the storms ahead.

When I was 16, Pearl Harbor was bombed. Furious that someone would pull a sneaky attack on my beloved country, I tried to join the Navy but was sent home to "grow a little more." I finally enlisted in March of 1943 and ended up in the North Atlantic on submarine patrol aboard the *USS Muskegon*.

I remember there were times when I thought I couldn't possibly take another night on deck in the freezing spray or another call to our battle stations.

But when the spray was the coldest, the night the blackest and home as far away as it could be, I'd remember those silly flowered shirts and tell myself, *If I survived those battles at recess, I can survive this.*

Now, over 50 years later, my recollections of the recesses, the shirts and the North Atlantic are clear as ever.

In fact, I married the girl who used to watch me take on those toughies at school. Sometimes I wonder if those "flower power" battles were what won her for me.

good memories were in the bag

"We lived in a small mining town when I was growing up," writes Rosemary Peterson of Fernley, Nevada. "This picture of my sisters and me (center) was taken on Easter in 1936. My mother would save the prettiest prints from the feed sacks for our Easter dresses and always made panties to match. She made up her own patterns and sewed them on an old Singer treadle machine. We had such fun picking out the patterns for our school dresses. Even though times were hard, I always look at this picture of the three of us with fondness and good memories."

When visions of lollypops dance in her head...
she's dreaming of Avon's **Miss Lollypop** fragrance group!

Meet Miss Lollypop: Avon's happy new fragrance for young ladies. She's a spirited personality in cool Cologne Mist, Splash Cologne, silky Cream Sachet, smooth Soap and Sponge, fluffy Talc and Puff...so many grown-up fragrance forms.

Your Avon Representative always has wonderful fragrance ideas for everyone in your family. Do ask her about new Miss Lollypop —and make a little girl's dream come true!

AVON
cosmetics
ROCKEFELLER PLAZA, NEW YORK
©1967 Avon Products, Inc.

1967

hair-raising memories

WHO HASN'T BEEN TEASED BY CHILDREN OR GRANDCHILDREN WHEN THEY CATCH A GLIMPSE OF THE 'DOS WE DONNED AS KIDS?

IT WASN'T PERMANENT. "For my first day of school in 1949, I knew I'd have a new permanent," says Susan Daniels Gaskins of Stonewall, North Carolina. "I'm not sure what I hated most, my red hair or my new perm."

HIS SUNDAY BEST—AND WORST. "As an 8-year-old in 1946, I had mixed feelings about Sundays," admits Richard Haywood, Laurel, Maryland. "While Dad's traditional dinner of chicken and mashed potatoes still makes my mouth water, I dreaded dressing up in a suit and tie for church and having Dad comb my red hair and part it!"

86

Growing Up

THIS LITTLE PIGTAIL.
"Here is my favorite photo of myself," confesses Ginny La Bar from Riegelsville, Pennsylvania. "Growing up in the 1950s in Houston, Texas, I loved my pigtails—can you tell?"

teen was a victim of trend

For some reason, understood only by a 15-year-old, I just had to have my long hair cut. We were living on a farm in Mahomet, Illinois, during the Depression, and Dad was the official barber in our household.

I wanted the latest in-fashion haircut, but I felt uneasy as I watched my hair pile up on the floor. When Dad was done, I rushed to the mirror to view my updated look.

What I saw was a 2-inches-above-the-neck shingle that was the latest fad in 1929. The problem was, this was 1937!

My worst nightmare had happened. My life was ruined forever! I lost my temper, threw the hand mirror across the room—for which I received a sound scolding—then ran out sobbing.

Mom let me calm down, then gradually convinced me there was hope. She heated the curling iron in the oil lamp and curled locks of hair on top of my head.

Persuaded by Mom that I looked cute and would probably set a new style at Mahomet High School, I anxiously greeted my beau of the moment when he came calling in his red Model A.

Imagine my reaction when I opened the door and he blurted out, "Good grief! You look like a peeled onion!" I let forth a wail and ran upstairs to my room.

Mom again came to the rescue with a close-fitting cap, which I wore for a month until my hair grew long enough, and I had saved the $3 needed to get a permanent.

—*Alice Lange, Prescott, Arizona*

CUTE 'N' CURLY. Pin curls were popular in the '50s, as Nancy Krampert showed in 1958. "Mother trimmed my hair every so often," says Nancy, of Bayville, New Jersey. "I specifically remember her cutting my bangs crooked, then trying to even them up until they were almost up to my hairline. Thank goodness for hairdressers!"

corkscrew curls carried a painful price

By Donna Williams, Waukesha, Wisconsin

R-I-I-I-I-P! Rip! Rip! R-i-i-i-i-p! Whenever I heard that familiar tearing sound on Saturday nights, I knew exactly what it meant—a pile of rags in front of Mom and a painful headful of "wiener curls" for me.

The Saturday night bath was a regular part of my weekly routine when I was growing up in West Allis, Wisconsin, in the early '40s.

Once out of the tub, I dressed in one of my favorite nighties and put on knitted slippers. Then I heard the dreaded sound again. Rip! Rip! R-i-i-i-i-p! Oh, that sound

hurt my ears, but I knew my head would hurt more before long!

When the tearing sound finally stopped, Mom beckoned me into the dining room. I sat at the table, with a torn pile of rags in front of me.

I recognized the fabric as one of my former bedsheets, now perfectly ripped into strips about 1 inch by 12 inches in size.

The first step of this horrid ritual was for my damp hair to be combed, and then divided into eight sections.

A rag was placed next to a length of sectioned hair. Mom tugged at my scalp as she twisted the hair and the rag tightly together from hair end to scalp. Then she'd bend it up and move onto the next section.

Each rag was painstakingly put into place until the last hair section was wrapped. As I looked down, I saw that the pile of rags in front of me looked hardly touched. Oh, no—enough for another night!

Carefully, Mom stretched an elastic headband around the collection of corkscrews. That uncomfortable headband had to stay in place while I slept, and Mom firmly reminded me not to fuss with it, or the curls would not turn out. Never mind that sleeping was next to impossible.

I found myself looking forward to the morning. It wasn't the excitement of all the attention my "wiener curls" would attract—it was a longing for the release of that vise-like headband and the unwrapping of the corkscrews.

shirley temple style

"As this 1945 photo shows, my mother liked to keep my sister Joyce and me in Shirley Temple curls," writes Joan Smith of Oakhurst, California. "I remember Mom's fingernails pressing against my head as she wound my wet hair around her finger. Then she'd secure the curls with bobby pins until my hair was dry."

FOR 35 YEARS
BUSTER BROWN HAS HELPED MANY A TODDLER GROW TO TEEN AGE

The Show-off

Now ready with the smartest styles in Buster Brown history

Many a little tot has proudly taken new Buster Browns to bed with him. Many a girl, trembling on the brink of her teens, has danced her first dance in organdie and Buster Browns. And the satisfied self-consciousness of an eight-year-old in new Buster Browns is happy to see.

Since 1904, these things have happened. Maybe you, Mother, grew up in Buster Browns. And maybe your husband shinnied up the old apple tree in these famous shoes.

For youngsters, the big thing about Busters is "My-but-aren't-I-grown-up" styles. Big folks styles adapted for the *youngest* set. You used to like that, too.

As parents you look to other things.

Our sixty-year-old company has been making Buster Brown Shoes for generations of children. And since 'Way Back When' we have put emphasis on *wear* and *fit*.

But health features endeared this trademark to mothers perhaps more than anything else. Gentle support for tender ankles and arches. Aids to keeping toes straight as Nature intended. Cushioning for the jarring shocks of youngsters coming down hard on

Back to School Time is Buster Brown Time . . . and Buster Brown has just the healthful Grown-Up Styles to make those young, growing feet happier as they walk and run.

their heels. Or any of the many other health ideas that Busters pioneered.

There's a store in your city now featuring the new Buster Brown styles in a complete range of sizes and lasts. Take in the children for their fall shoes. BROWN SHOE COMPANY, St. Louis. *Also makers of Buster Brown Official Boy Scout and Buster Brown Official Girl Scout Shoes.*

BUSTER BROWN
SHOES
FOR GIRLS AND BOYS OF ALL AGES

1939

he stepped out in style

FOLLOWING FASHION DOESN'T ALWAYS MEAN PUTTING YOUR BEST FOOT FORWARD.

In 1939, when I was in seventh grade, our junior high school decided to start a band. Our teacher and all the mothers got together to come up with a uniform. The school board provided maroon-and-gray chintz fabric from which the moms sewed capes and berets. Each student had to buy a shirt, duck slacks and shoes

With money in hand, I walked four miles to the local Thom McAn store, where I eyed a pair of shoes I just had to have—brown-and-white moccasins with crepe soles. They were too small for me, but they sure were sharp, and the $3.45 price was just right.

On the day of the parade, I proudly put on my new uniform and fashion-forward footwear. After walking about a quarter of a mile, the soles of my feet were on fire, my toes were cramping and my heels were blistering. By the end of our march, I was practically on my hands and knees. Those beautiful but ill-fitting shoes made their first and last appearance on my feet that day!

—*Edward Bjorkman, DeFuniak Springs, Florida*

a pair with parasols

"Growing up during the Depression with divorced parents, my older sister Virginia and I were the best of friends," writes Jerry Priddy of Edmond, Oklahoma. "Our dad took this 1935 picture of us when we were living in Independence, Kansas. At 7 and 5 years old, we were so proud of our pretty parasols and pocketbooks, but especially of our high-button shoes!"

made with love by mom

STORE-BOUGHT CLOTHES WERE NO MATCH FOR MOM'S.

CAP AND COAT. "My mother, Hazel Snider, fashioned this hat and coat from clothes she bought secondhand," says Dorothy Everds of Leland, North Carolina. "My dad, Warren, took the photo in 1934, when I was 8. We lived in Cleveland then. Dad loved photography and always carried a camera."

WINDOWS TO THE PAST

I open my scrapbook to relive the scenes from my childhood of the 1940s and '50s in New York City, closing my eyes and imagining the moment, place and time.

Among them is this one of me (middle) holding the hands of my sisters, Irene (left) and Helen Mitchell, in the mid-1940s.

No one could be more fashionable than we three sisters. Mom made all three of our matching outfits of black-and-white checkered material, with pleated skirts and hats to match.

Many years later, I carefully wrote underneath that photograph, in my scrapbook, "Anne Bancroft (Irene), Ginger Rogers (me, the dancer) and Audrey Hepburn (Helen, the model type)."

I never underestimate the power of just one black-and-white or early color photograph to take me home again.

—*Carolyn Mitchell Rhodes, Tuscaloosa, Alabama*

IN THEIR EASTER BONNETS. Fancy new spring outfits were once practically a requirement for Easter. "In 1947, Mother made matching bonnets and dresses for my sister, Charlene (right), and me," recalls JoAnn Cooke of Reseda, California.

CROCHETED CUTIE. "Mother was very talented and made most of my clothes, including this crocheted dress," says Ruth Gensimore of Alexandria, Pennsylvania. The studio portrait was taken in 1937 or '38.

CARIBBEAN COUTURE. "My mother, Frances, often sewed clothes for my two brothers and me," says Jack Seagrove of El Paso, Texas. "You can see she was influenced by the Caribbean music of Harry Belafonte when she made this outfit for me in 1957, when I was about 8 years old."

salute to heroes

THE CLOTHES KIDS LOVED TO WEAR THE MOST REFLECTED THEIR
AFFECTION FOR FAVORITE ACTION FIGURES AND REAL-LIFE WARRIORS.

READY FOR THE RODEO. "Our family jumped into Southern culture when we moved from New York to Alabama in 1954," recalls Robert Pringle, Montgomery, Alabama. "Here sons Glen and Gary don cowboy attire for a day at the rodeo."

QUICK-DRAW ARTISTS
"My sons, Ken (left) and Bob, were 2 and 3 when they modeled their cowboy outfits in 1953," relates Leslie Hunt from Berlin, Wisconsin. "My father, Leslie 'Bud' Webster, took the picture at his home in North St. Paul, Minnesota, where we all lived at the time. Ken is wearing his Jumping Jack shoes, a popular brand that I bought for all four of my children."

"Here I am wearing my 'Lucky Lindy' cap in 1932. I was on my way home from school," notes Friel Hall of Carmel, Indiana. "Charles Lindbergh was a hero to all of us American boys in those days."

MEN IN UNIFORM. "I was so taken by my uncle Loren Nauss' Army uniform in 1944, my mother made one for me and we posed for this picture at our home, in Brighton, Michigan," writes James Young of Hazel Green, Alabama. "I guess my fondness for military uniforms continued, as I spent 23 years in the Air Force and 16 more as a civilian working for the Army."

NAVY STRIPES.
"This photograph of my brother Tom (right) and me was taken in May of 1942, when we were ages 3 and 5," writes Jon King of Stanwood, Washington. "Little did we or family and friends know at the time that I would end up a sailor in the U.S. Coast Guard."

fashion flashback

ALL DRESSED UP. "Besides our one-piece wool bathing suits in the late '20s and early '30s, we wore white rubber bathing slippers and bathing caps," recalls Dorothy Ives McChesney (right), Moriah, New York. "The swimming hole was near Troy, New York, where the Poestenkill and Quackenkill creeks met. Also in the picture are (from left) my sisters Marjorie and Ruth and our cousin Audrey Schmay. We changed into our bathing suits in the car. Mother made orange floral cretonne curtains for the car windows."

TOUGH AS NAILS FOR TYKES. "The sueded cotton cloth of the Klad-Ezee Baby Tweener being modeled by my son, Eric, in 1967 was a perfect weight for spring and fall," remembers Janice Korpela of Cornucopia, Wisconsin. "The one-piece outfit was tough, too—all four of my children wore it at some point."

> ## "A sister is a little bit of childhood that can never be lost."
> —MARION C. GARRETH

the last boy in knickers

By Michael Remas
Williamsport, Pennsylvania

During the 1940s, I reached the conclusion that I was probably the last kid in the area who still wore knickers. It was a distinction I didn't enjoy.

As a 12-year-old boy, I was embarrassed. My pals usually sported long pants when we gathered to play ball. But according to my parents, simply discarding the knickers because fashions had changed was a waste. Clothes were meant to be worn out or outgrown. So I suffered in silence until the day my life as the neighborhood knickers kid neared an end.

My friend Billy Barney and I were walking down the street when a neighbor's dog began barking at us. We ignored him, but suddenly he charged at us. Billy ran, and I climbed on top of a small coal shed—but I wasn't quick enough. The mutt bit one leg of my knickers, giving it a good rip. Eventually, I was able to shake him loose, and he trotted away.

While I was happy that my knickers had suffered a potentially fatal injury, I was afraid Mom wouldn't believe the true tale of the dog. But she did, and she said I couldn't play in torn knickers. *At long last,* I thought, *I'll be able to go around in long pants, just like my buddies!*

No such luck. My parents bought me a pair of blue bib overalls. Now I looked like Li'l Abner. The only solution was to wear my shirt over the top—and to go searching for that fashion-crazy canine.

APRON STRINGS. Aprons were a practical kitchen fashion that came in all patterns and colors, as shown in 1960 by Barbara (left) and Carolyn Clark, daughters of Janet Clark from Fort Worth, Texas.

DAPPER TOPPERS. "This picture of my brothers, 4-year-old Thomas Marron (left) and 5-year-old Frank, was shot in 1951 in Danbury, Connecticut, 'Hat Capital of the World,' in the 1950s," writes Paula Marron of Danbury. "All the boys and men wore hats there. The photo was taken before we went to church one Easter Sunday, and Frank had marbles in his pocket."

TRIO OF POODLES. "My three daughters, Anita, Patty and Christine, are wearing the pink poodle skirts and navy blue tops they got from their grandparents one Christmas in the '50s," recalls Mary Brown of Prophetstown, Illinois. "At first, the girls thought the outfits were cute. But after Patty outgrew hers and had to wear her sisters' as hand-me-downs, she didn't think so."

1960S MOD. "This slide from July of 1966 shows me in my '60s-style dress of dark brown circles," writes Carol Burghauser of Rosedale, Maryland. "The dress always reminds me of Marlo Thomas and the fashions she wore on her television show from the era, *That Girl*."

FURRY FASHION. "Davy Crockett was all the rage when my oldest brother, John Michael—'Mike'—turned 2 in 1955," notes Tara Houghton of Dorothy, New Jersey. "In this photo with our mom, Jane Wilkinson, Mike proudly wears a Davy Crockett hat to the breakfast table."

oh, brother

"When I was young, my brothers and I had to wear knickers,
suit coats and an occasional hat when we went somewhere special,"
writes Dick Mortenson of Stow, Massachusetts. The photo shows
(from left) Bob, David and Dick heading off to church in 1942.

CHAPTER FIVE

Kidding Around

With the constant fear that Mom would give them a long list of chores, kids did anything to avoid uttering the phrase, "I'm bored!" So, long before the days of video games, cable TV and computers, young ones quickly found ways to entertain themselves for hours on end. Sometimes it took nothing more than a few everyday items and a little imagination to make endearing memories that lasted forever.

"My two brothers and I had a wonderful childhood in a residential area called Lansdowne Park," recalls Lois Pethick McDonald of Wysox, Pennsylvania. "The kids in our tight-knit community remained close all through the school years.

"In the summer of 1941, when I was 9 years old, my brother, Dick, started a kazoo marching band. In the photo below right, 10-year-old Dick is sitting on the ground, and I'm the majorette in the middle.

"The group practiced in a vacant lot and even enlisted our dog as the mascot. Proudly wearing hats made from oatmeal boxes, we marched up and down the streets, buzzing happily on our kazoos!"

Dressing up, listening to the radio, enjoying the outdoors, watching movies...turn the page and see if these memories strike a chord with you.

tuned in to entertainment

By Pauline Vetter
Fairfax, Virginia

Listening to three or four mystery shows on the radio on Sunday evenings in Chicago was a very special family time for me and my parents, Howard and Doris Parmen, back in the 1940s.

We would have a great big dinner around 1 o'clock in the afternoon, usually fried chicken, mashed potatoes and gravy.

Then, around 5 o'clock, we'd munch on popcorn or fudge, but we'd never sit at the table while we listened to our programs. Mother enjoyed being out of the kitchen Sunday evenings.

We had a special popcorn kettle with a crank on top to stir from the outside. The kettle's universal cord was also used for the family iron and toaster and about four other electrical appliances. If you left the hot iron too close to the cloth-covered cord, it would begin to singe. Soon, you would see the wire inside and have to buy a new cord.

The pretty tablecloth in the picture (opposite, top) was ironed with a mangle, which was heated with gas and had big rollers like a wringer washing machine.

Mom always had nicely folded tablecloths.

Our radio was a Scott, and each tube in back had a chrome casing around it. It was a nice radio, a beautiful piece of furniture, and had an overseas band on it.

The 30-minute radio mysteries we listened to included *The Shadow, I Love a Mystery, This Is Your FBI* and *Inner Sanctum Mysteries.* We all liked the mysteries, Dad and I especially.

I was only 6 years old in 1942, but I remember I was always waiting for Margo to figure out why Lamont was never there to talk to the Shadow.

I remember those Sundays and radio shows so well. They were part of simpler times.

SUNDAY TRADITION. After Pauline Vetter helped dad Howard Parmen pop corn in the kitchen, they joined her mother, Doris, around the Scott radio for the Sunday serials.

he was a rascal over the airwaves

HAMMING IT UP ON AMATEUR RADIO LED TO A LIFELONG PASSION.

By Henry Canvel, Las Vegas, Nevada

My first experience with ham radio was when I was a ninth-grader in Los Angeles. I built my first five-meter radio transceiver (a combined transmitter and receiver) and was able to communicate with amateur radio operators within a 40-mile radius. It felt like worlds away! But I wasn't aware others were listening as well.

One day after school, my mother met me at the door and told me a man was waiting for me. He had cut all the wires on my transceiver. Because I didn't have an amateur radio operator license, I was subject to a $10,000 fine or 10 years in prison. Gulp! After a stern lecture, I promised never to do it again.

Well, a few months later, I couldn't resist plunging into my next project—building a more powerful 160-meter transmitter in a wooden prune box. I stretched a long wire across our tile roof between two poles for the antenna, and modified an old radio to tune to the 160-meter band. The first time I fired up the transmitter, a friend four miles away called me to say he was listening to me over the airwaves. That was it—I was hooked!

I became bolder. After toying around with the operating frequencies, I was able to communicate on the bandwidth for the Los Angeles Police Department. One night, a friend and I took my primitive prune-box transmitter up to the old "Hollywoodland" sign—it now says simply "Hollywood." In those days, the sign was illuminated by 4,000 20-watt lightbulbs. My friend and I removed one of the bulbs and, with an adapter, powered the transmitter. I strung a wire up for the antenna and tuned the transmitter to the LAPD frequency.

The first time I fired up the transmitter, a friend four miles away called me to say he was listening to me over the airwaves. That was it—I was hooked!

I proceeded to direct police car 33W, the patrol car in our Silverlake neighborhood, to a phony address and told them to go jump in the lake. Although my friend and I continued our shenanigans a bit longer, the thought of getting caught again finally scared me off the hill.

But that schoolboy obsession lasted throughout my life. Eventually, my childhood pranks led to my Navy assignment of recording the signing of the peace treaty with Japan at the end of World War II. Now, *that* was worth tuning in for!

a boy and his radio

Radio made my imagination come alive, and the photo above captures the enjoyment and education I received from the variety of music, news coverage and storytelling transmitted over the airwaves throughout the 1930s and '40s.

I was 4 years old when the picture was taken, in 1936, at our duplex in Los Angeles. The multicolored leather hassock that I'm sitting on was a common front room accessory in homes, at least on the West Coast. It was used as an impromptu ottoman, a substitute chair or a place to confine shedding house pets—sort of the pets' authorized throne.

My favorite song at the time was *The Whistler and His Dog*. It was a theme song for a midafternoon program called *The Johnson Family*, which entertained our mothers and signaled that it was time for my afternoon snack.

As an only child, I found the radio one of my favorite companions, treating me to a stimulating repertoire of music, drama and world news. It remains so to this day, even after many years of being happily married with three grown children.

—Bob Rogers, Pasadena, California

New! **HOPALONG CASSIDY RADIO** by Arvin

$16⁹⁵ With Lariatenna Underwriters' Listed

William Boyd as Hopalong Cassidy, idol of American kids!

Model 441T

1950

the silver screen was enticing

SATURDAY MATINEE BUFF

Growing up as an only child in the 1930s (right), I found movies to be good company.

I had a paper route, which paid for my movie ticket, the streetcar ride to and from the Saturday afternoon matinee and popcorn with real butter—a nickel a sack.

The matinee usually began with a double feature. Sometimes, during a suspenseful part of the show, someone would blow up a paper bag and pop it just to hear the girls scream.

Then came a color cartoon, previews of coming attractions and a chapter from a serial, which ended with a cliff-hanger that coaxed people to come back the following Saturday.

My favorite part of the matinee was the serial. The characters I liked best were Flash Gordon, Dick Tracy, the Phantom, Mandrake the Magician, the Shadow and the Spider.

When it was time to go, I'd reach into my pocket for my streetcar fare home. One time, I discovered my coins were gone. The lady in the

seat next to mine, sensing my predicament, reached into her purse and gave me a dime. I was a very relieved youngster accepting the kindness of a stranger.

—*William Apple, Little Rock, Arkansas*

CAPTIVATED KIDS.
Like so many youngsters, these kids are entranced with the movie being shown on the big screen in front of them.

SUPERSTOCK

Growing Up

lost in the magic of the movies

IT WAS EASY TO LOSE TRACK OF TIME BACK IN THE DAYS WHEN YOU COULD SIT THROUGH A MOVIE TWO OR EVEN THREE TIMES.

By Marlene Hickey, Mission Viejo, California

There were two movie theaters in Scottsbluff, Nebraska, where I grew up in the '40s. Every week I went to at least two shows. If no one else in my family could go, I went alone.

Both movie houses were located downtown on Broadway, about two miles from home. We had no car and walked everywhere, so that didn't seem far. On cold days, or when dusk came early, I was given 20 cents to take a cab home.

On Saturday afternoons, we kids went to the Oto Theater, which had an Indian chief's head above the entrance. For the 5-cent admission, we could watch a cartoon, a serial and the feature, usually a Western. One matinee was particularly memorable. The first 50 kids received a 5-cent candy bar. That made the movie free!

The Oto was old, and some kids claimed mice scampered across their feet. It never happened to me—not that I'd have noticed.

If a mouse had jumped onto the armrest and helped itself to my popcorn, I probably would not have known. I usually identified so strongly with someone in the movie that it took me a long time to step out of character once the movie ended.

On Sundays, I accompanied my family to the Egyptian, a theater for more serious fare, where the admission was an expensive 10 cents.

The Egyptian was ornate, with carpets, a great velvet curtain and a lounge featuring overstuffed furniture and Egyptian artifacts.

One day I went to the Egyptian alone and saw the tearjerker *Penny Serenade*, starring Cary Grant and Irene Dunne. The couple's unborn baby dies; then after they adopt, that child dies. In the happy ending, they again adopt a child.

I thought I'd die as I watched the movie. I wept buckets and knew I had to see it again.

Between showings, I sat in the second-floor lounge. As I waited, I glanced out the window at the town, where it was still daylight. I had no watch, since few children wore them then. I figured it was still early afternoon, forgetting it was summer and stayed light until very late in the day.

For the third time, I sat huddled in my front-row seat, staring up at the screen, suffering along with Cary and Irene, when the voice of my brother, Charles, sounded in my ear.

"Just what do you think you're doing?" he demanded. "It's 9 o'clock. Mom and Dad are scared to death. They've even had the police looking all over town for you."

The family had checked the theater three times, but because I always sat scrunched down in the first row, they'd missed seeing me.

After my first, and only, spanking, I was sent to bed without supper. That was fine. The spanking was not that bad, and Mom later smuggled some food up to me.

But I needed no food, as my spirit had been nourished by the movie and those beautiful people on the screen who had spoken just to me.

LITTLE BREADWINNER.
"Our son, Donald, was just a toddler, but he never missed *Bandstand*, which is what the local Philadelphia show was called before it went national as *American Bandstand*," writes Arline Quigley of Pipersville, Pennsylvania. "One February afternoon in 1955, I left the room to do some chores. When I came back, Donald was in the same position, but with an opened loaf of bread!"

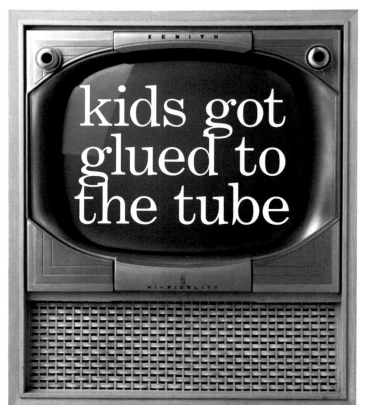

kids got glued to the tube

WHAT TIME IS IT?
"It was about 1955, and we were at a fair in Waterford, Connecticut, a small town near New London," Mary Suominen of Scottsdale, Arizona, remembers. "We walked around the large stage set up for the entertainment, and there was Howdy Doody! The man lifted my daughter, Sue, onto the stage and let her hold Howdy on her lap for this photo." Sue, now Susan Barton of St. Augustine, Florida, adds, "Having my arms around that famous Howdy Doody puppet was like being next to a movie star. It was so exciting!"

do-bee-have

WATCHING *ROMPER ROOM* IN '64 CREATED
A TEMPORARY TRUCE FOR THREE SIBLINGS.

As a 4-year-old girl in 1964, I sat glued to the television watching my favorite show, *Romper Room*, every morning.

I always had to watch the show sandwiched between my older brother, 5, and my pesky 3-year-old sister. It was the only time we were all in the same room and not bickering.

Miss Sally, along with a lucky group of "TV kids," would show us how to brush our teeth, pick up toys and do all the things a good Do Bee should. She would also sing songs about bad behavior so we could be sure to avoid it.

At the end of the show, Miss Sally would peer into the camera and hold up her Magic Mirror, and we'd drown each other out reciting, "Romper bomper, stomper boo. Tell me, tell me, tell me do. Magic Mirror, tell me today. Did all my friends have fun at play?"

We got quiet as mice as she continued…

"I see Susie and Debbie and Cathy. Look, there's Diane and Mary and Dennis and Johnny. I hope you all had fun today. Bye-bye, Do Bees!"

My siblings, Dennis and Diane, would whoop with joy at the sweet sounds of their names while I'd grab my Chatty Cathy doll and go off and pout in a corner.

"Oh, Darlene, Do Bee a big girl. Don't Bee a pout," Dennis would say.

"Maybe someday Miss Sally will see you," Diane said as she tried to pat me on the head and snatch my doll at the same time.

I could watch *Romper Room* till I was old and I'd never hear my name. This was Mom's fault!

I ran into the kitchen to confront her. "Mommy, why did you name me Darlene? Why not Mary or Susie or Cathy?" I whined.

"Well, honey, Daddy and I couldn't decide between Debbie and Darlene. We put both names in a hat and picked out…"

"I know…*Darlene*," I frowned.

"No, actually we picked out Debbie," Mom laughed. "But we thought there were too many Debbies at the time, so we named you Darlene.

"It's a pretty name for a very pretty girl." She hugged me and planted a kiss on my cheek.

Having Mom's hugs all to myself was better than a Magic Mirror any day.

—*Darlene Totzke Buechel, Chilton, Wisconsin*

BE A DO BEE.
On *Romper Room*, teachers like Miss Nancy (Miss Sally's daughter and TV successor) inspired a generation of youngsters to mind their P's and Q's.

FUNNIES WERE A TREAT
We got a Sunday paper only once in a while, so it was a big treat. On this Sunday in 1945, my dad, Edgar Wussler, my sister, Marilyn, 8, and I, 4, were very intent on reading the paper on our back porch in St. Charles, Missouri. That's my 2-year-old brother, Donald, looking through the screen door.

—*Lorita Thornhill, St. Peters, Missouri*

> *For children, play is serious learning. Play is really the work of children.*
>
> — FRED ROGERS

Kidding Around

PACK-O-FUN MAGAZINE was first published in 1951 by Edna Clapper, a den mother who developed project ideas for her Cub Scout troop. The crafts were designed to be inexpensive so they'd fit the budgets of Scout leaders, teachers and mothers. Thanks to Alice Jena of Richmond Hill, New York, for sharing.

25c

MAY
1960

Just for FUN

Here's tin can stilts and pictures gay, doll house book and

USE FOR PER DOLLS

T V SHOW

House for Pap...
The walls of your c... made from sheets of stif... paper. Punch holes and... together loosely, as if m... book. Glue magazine... various rooms onto the... up the book, open the... your paper dolls into a... wish.

TV Show
Cut an opening for th... in one side of envelope... catalog or magazine has b... Draw dials for tuning... on the tips of your finger... your hand inside.

CAN STILTS

Tin Can Stilts
You will need two tall... cans and two pieces of r... feet long. Use a hammer a... punch two opposite holes i... near the closed end. Inser... through the holes and tie... together. You can paint y... if you wish.
Step on closed ends of... hold rope in your hands... lift your foot, pull on the r...

Thumbtack Picture...
Use a piece of corrugat... board from grocery cartons... background. Sketch the desig... "painted" and insert thumb... intervals along the lines. Tie... of white or colored string arou... of the tacks and wind it around the others in sequence. Tie string to final thumbtack.

ACK PICTURES

BACKYARD GAMES

Obstacle Catch
Here's a different way to play catch! Stand with a tree between players and toss the ball on either side. Keep tossing back and forth without moving your feet.

Sidewalk Shadows
This is fun to do on a sunny day. While you make a shadow on the sidewalk, your friend can draw a face on the shadow with chalk and add a costume — hat, collar and so on. Make your arms and legs move so the shadow character puts on a dance.

Pebble Toss
Place a pebble on the back of your hand. Toss it up and catch it with your palm. Now try two, three, or more pebbles. The one who can catch the most is the winner.

Clothesline Tennis
Wad up a double sheet of news-paper into a ball and fasten it by wrapping with cellophane tape. Cut a paddle from grocery carton card-board about 5" x 12". Stand on one side of the clothesline and bat the ball over the line. Before the ball hits the ground, run under the line and bat it back to the original side. Keep it up until you miss.

Mailing Tube Gun
Near one end of a mailing tube, cut a hole large enough for your thumb. Place your thumb in the hole and drop a small rubber ball in the tube. Aim the gun by raising it against your shoulder and then flip-ping it forward. Practice trying to make the ball go inside a basket or box placed in your back yard.

MAY 1960

OBSTACLE CATCH

SIDEWALK SHADOWS

CLOTHESLINE TENNIS

MAILING TUBE GUN

winter, spring summer, fall
Kids sure do have a ball!

ICY SITUATION. Skating was a wonderful way for kids in colder climates to while away winter days. "This 1962 photo of my daughters Sandy, 6, and Linda, 9, was taken at a local park," says Michael Lacivita of Youngstown, Ohio. "You don't see skates like the ones Sandy is wearing anymore!"

TREE FORT FOR ALL. "After Christmas, my brother and his friends would round up all the neighbors' discarded Christmas trees and build a fort in the yard of our home on the south side of Chicago," recalls Louise Freitag of Oak Park, Illinois. "In this 1952 photo, it looks as if we're ready to start a snowball fight! Pictured, from left, are neighbor Mary Green; my brother, Jim; me; and my sister, Ann."

batter up!

"The East Danvers (Massachusetts) Red Sox team was organized by my father, Arthur Balser Sr. (back row, right)," relates Bernie Balser (front row, second from right) of Salem.

"We had uniforms, which my generous dad bought for several of the players, but we wore plain sneakers or regular shoes. The bats were taped so we could hold onto them better.

"What a team it was. Nobody in the Danvers or Salem area could beat us that summer of 1949. My brother Art (second row, center) was the pitcher and the star of the team. I played second base.

" 'Dudsy' Dowdell (second row, far right) became a star on the high school team a few years later.

"I'll never forget how itchy those wool uniforms were. We'd sweat buckets within minutes of playing. But it was a blast!"

SLEDDING ON SNOWY DAYS

I grew up in the little town of Paden City, nestled in the beautiful hills of West Virginia along the Ohio River. When several inches of snow covered the ground each winter, my two brothers, cousins, neighbor friends and I would race to get our sleds and prepare them for the season.

Using paraffin, I would wax the runners of my Fleetwood Racer so that it would fly over the snow. Then we'd blaze a trail through the woods until we came to the nearby open pasture. With a running start, we'd throw the sleds on the ground, land on our bellies and head down the hill. By the time we went down the first hill and up and over the next one, we were really flying! To avoid ending up on the highway, we'd drag our feet and turn our sleds, which meant a tumble into the snow. But that just added to the fun!

Then we'd head back up the hill for another run. Sometimes we would ride double, with one person lying on another's back. Before reaching the bottom of the second hill, the person on top would fall off and get a face full of snow. Our sled rides would last for hours, usually until long after I had lost feeling in my hands and feet.

—*Lesta Wells, Middlebourne, West Virginia*

SPLISHIN' AND SPLASHIN' IN SUMMER

"Our parents, Raymond and Emma, saw to it that my three siblings and I had plenty to do during the summer of 1939, even if it meant spending a bit of money," recalls Regina Ehrhardt of Rushville, Illinois. "For $12.36, they bought a little wading pool and a child-size canvas grocery tent from the Hettrick Manufacturing Co. of Toldeo, Ohio. I still have the receipt!"

In the photo below, Regina's brother, Donald, and a neighbor girl are manning the grocery store, while sisters Barbara (far left), Cecilia (middle) and infant Regina keep their cool in the pool with two friends. A neighbor prefers to stay dry and serve as lifeguard.

Wading Pool and Beach Toys made by Urb Plastics Corp., New York

1950

WIENIE ROASTS WERE BIG FUN.
"We used to have neighborhood parties cooking wienies and marshmallows over an open fire in Willow Park in Des Plaines," writes Nancy Siria of Arlington Heights, Illinois. "This photo was taken in 1949. My sister Judy is the little girl perched on the neighbor's knee."

WORK AND PLAY. "This slide was taken by our father, Wilson Himes, in front of our home in Kane, Pennsylvania, in '51," recalls Sylvia Glans, who now resides in Cochranton. "My twin sister, Cindy, 9, is in the pile of leaves that I raked. We thought raking leaves was lots of fun. A game we played in our backyard involved raking the fallen leaves into lines for rooms and playing house."

costumes weren't just for Halloween

Who needed a reason to dive into the dress-up bin and don a costume? With a quick change of clothes, you could transform yourself into a different person!

HEROES OF THE WEST. Make that the Midwest, as these two boys dressed in authentic-looking gear lived in Joliet, Illinois. "This picture of my older brothers was taken around 1931," explains Ida Alexander of Bishopville, South Carolina. "Oliver Johnson is the cowboy on the left, at about age 8, and Sam is the 4-year-old American Indian. I was a toddler at the time."

MOM'S CAST-OFFS. "I loved to play dress-up in Mom's old clothes," recalls Cathy Wilkerson Jones of Rowlett, Texas. "Here I am in 1960, at age 9, in front of our neighbor's house in Garland, Texas. The neighbor lady made ceramics, and she would let me come in and watch. She donated the items she made to groups to sell at fund-raisers. She was very kind and patient, so I was over there a lot."

the swing

How do you like to go up in a swing,
Up in the air so blue?
Oh, I do think it the pleasantest thing
Ever a child can do!

Up in the air and over the wall,
Till I can see so wide,
Rivers and trees and cattle and all
Over the countryside—

Till I look down on the garden green,
Down on the roof so brown—
Up in the air I go flying again,
Up in the air and down!

—*Robert Louis Stevenson*

cale street kids were serious about having fun

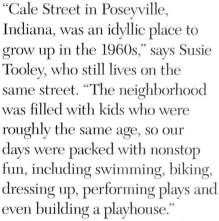

"Cale Street in Poseyville, Indiana, was an idyllic place to grow up in the 1960s," says Susie Tooley, who still lives on the same street. "The neighborhood was filled with kids who were roughly the same age, so our days were packed with nonstop fun, including swimming, biking, dressing up, performing plays and even building a playhouse."

These images were taken by E. Mott Wade, the father of Susie's best friend and neighbor, Shelley Glover, who now lives in Owensville, Indiana.

EARLY ENTREPRENEURS.
"We were always selling something," writes Shelley. "In this photo, I think we're peddling our treasured Cracker Jack prizes." Pictured, from left, are Tim, Susie, Shelley and Sharon Reising."We also raised money by putting on plays and charging admission," Susie adds. "Once we gave the money to the John F. Kennedy Library. I still have the thank-you note they sent us."

HOUSING PROJECT.

"After much begging on my part, Dad, who was a contractor, gave me a small aluminum display door so we could build a house around it," says Shelley. "The house became a neighborhood project as word spread of its construction."

With Cheryl Lynn Hammelman looking on, Shelley paints the prized playhouse. "Once it was completed, we slept in it often," recalls Shelley. "Eventually, the roof collapsed under the weight of snow."

SLUMBERING SWEETIES.

"The neighbor girls loved slumber parties, and it appears we're actually sleeping in this photo! But that wasn't the case most times," says Susie. "We tried to stay awake because pranks were played on those who fell asleep first. Once I was the victim, and had toothpaste squirted onto my face. I woke up with big red welts." Top to bottom, this picture shows Susie, Carolyn Hopf, Sharon Reising and Shelley.

HOWDY, PARTNER.

"You can definitely see the influence of *Gunsmoke* in this 1964 snapshot," says Susie. "Like most boys of the time, my twin brother, Tim, loved cowboy hats and toy guns. Shelley (right) and I took dance lessons and were always dressing up."

SKATING FIGURE. Jean Sell was part of a figure-skating club in Paterson, New Jersey, in the '40s. She is fifth from the left in photo, as her club performed in a 1944 revue called "School Days." Jean doesn't skate now, but she still has her skates.

roller skating was the 'in thing' in the '40s

By Jean Sell, Jacksonville, Florida

When we were teenagers in Paterson, New Jersey, back in the '40s, roller skating was the "in thing" on Friday nights and Saturday and Sunday afternoons.

I belonged to the Paterson Recreation Figure Skating Club of the Roller Skating Rinks of America. Twice a year we put on a revue. The photo above shows a number we did in a 1944 revue called "School Days." We all wore beanies.

In 1945 and '46, the rinks in New Jersey and New York were asked to participate in a charity show, with all the proceeds going to the March of Dimes.

In one revue, each club represented a different country. We were China. I remember having to catch the train before 6 a.m. to get to Queens for our practice sessions.

We had many skaters who were as good as some of the professional ice skaters we see today. I think it's sad that roller skating has never been added to the Olympics.

I skated until I was in my mid-50s. I still have my skates and their metal case!

Growing Up

shady characters

Remember when kids used their imaginations to make their own fun? Joanne Kebbekus of Elkhorn, Wisconsin, certainly does. "My daughter, Brenda, and son, Dan, made a cozy little tent with an old blanket," says Joanne. Looks like a nice spot to find some shade on a sunny summer day.

CHAPTER SIX

Toys We Treasured

Keeping ourselves busy when we were young was child's play, thanks to precious dolls, trucks, bikes, marbles and more. The recollections of an adored toy remain alive and vivid, holding a special place in our childhood memories.

For many of us, those toys have long been discarded, although never forgotten. Others are lucky enough to have those keepsakes in their possession and cherish them to this day.

"I received my life-size Patti Playpal doll on my ninth birthday, in 1960," says Lani Vasileff of Minneapolis (shown in the photo at right). "I named her Wendy after the character in *Peter Pan*. She's been sitting in my bedroom in several homes since that day.

"She has a suitcase full of clothes—some new, some vintage—that I change with the seasons. I know she's worth some money, but I would never think of parting with her. After all these years, she's become a part of the family."

Read on for more memories about toys that shaped our youth...

receiving cinderella doll was like a fairy tale

By Jeanne Adelmann
Woodstock, Illinois

When I was 7 years old, in 1950, my grandmother took me to see the movie *Cinderella*. As the oldest sister to four brothers in a working-class family, I helped around the house a lot and instantly related to the character.

That Christmas, I discovered a large box with my name on it under our tree and eagerly ripped off the wrapping paper to see a lovely Cinderella doll smiling at me. She wore a beautiful blue dress, just like the one in the movie. The only thing that didn't seem right was that the doll's hair was brown. Everyone knew Cinderella had blond hair, like me. But I kept my thoughts secret because I loved my gift so much.

Eager to start playing the next day, I lifted Cinderella off my bed when, to my horror, her head fell off and rolled across the floor. Crying, I carried the headless doll to my mother.

Thinking on her feet, she said, "Don't worry. We'll send her to the doll hospital, where they'll fix her up in no time." A doll hospital? I had never heard of such a thing, but I was relieved Mom thought Cinderella could be fixed.

I went about my days, missing the times I could have been spending with my doll, and soon school started up again after Christmas vacation.

One day I came home to find Cinderella once again sitting on my bed. She was all in one piece! But that wasn't the only surprise for me. Cinderella now had blond hair. I was old enough to suspect the secret of Santa—and doll hospitals—and knew this couldn't be the same doll from Christmas. No matter—I loved her just the same!

HAIR COLOR CONFUSION.
Jeanne Adelmann happily poses with Cinderella before the doll's mysterious transformation.

Toys We Treasured

how we adored *our dolls*

LITTLE MOMS WERE IN THE MAKING WHEN YOUNG GIRLS CARED FOR THEIR BABY DOLLS.

ALL DOLLED UP. "Dolls topped the wish lists of my sister and me at Christmas in 1962," writes Emily Kelly of Macomb, Illinois. "Santa surprised Maureen, 7, with Tiny Thumbelina and me, 3, with Chatty Baby. I think one of the grown-ups was reaching out to admire my new dolly, which explains my look of apprehension as I hug her tight in this photo. I enjoyed Chatty Baby until the day I decided she needed a bath. She wasn't chatty after that."

TRULY PITIFUL. "I first set eyes on Poor Pitiful Pearl on Christmas Day in 1957, when I was 5," says Jacqueline Miraglia, Farmingville, New York. "She came dressed in a blue peasant dress with white polka dots with a red patch on it and a matching scarf. She also had a party dress. My dad took this picture of Pearl and me at our Brooklyn, New York, home. (Pearl's the one with the headband.) I was trying to mimic her face. In the '60s, my sister Corann teased Pearl's hair in a beehive, which was popular then. It took me years to get all the knots out. She now proudly sits on my guest bed in her original dress, showing off that sheepish smile that I first saw her with 50 years ago."

CRAZY FOR KIDDLES.
Measuring less than 4 inches tall, Mattel's Liddle Kiddle dolls kicked off a small-doll craze in the mid-1960s. Each doll came with a clever rhyming name and adorable themed accessories. The pint-size pals captured the hearts of little girls across the country, including Veronica Berger.

"I still have my Kiddle Klub House and the Liddle Kiddle dolls, including Peter Paniddle (next to Tinkerbell), Calamity Jiddle (on the rocking horse), Howard 'Biff' Boodle (in the red wagon) and Tracy Trikediddle (on the tricycle)," writes Veronica from Minneapolis.

loving the liddle kiddle dolls

Of all the toys I had while growing up in the 1960s, the Liddle Kiddle dolls were my favorite. For a solid five years, the only thing I asked for each Christmas and birthday was another Liddle Kiddle. By the time I was 10, I had collected more than 50 of them and even received the Kiddle Klub House.

As a lonely, shy little girl who had difficulty talking to other kids, I considered these tiny dolls my best friends. With my active imagination, I scripted screenplays that were loosely based on movies I'd seen and books I'd read. In my productions, I would make the dolls act out the scenes. When the setting was a jungle or a forest, my backyard was the perfect locale.

Occasionally, I would sneak one or two dolls with me to school as stowaways in my backpack. I would carefully hide them in my desk, away from my teacher's prying eyes.

My love of the theater continues today in the traveling troupe my husband and I operate. But instead of enlisting my Liddle Kiddles as characters, I now cast real people to perform in my productions!

—*Veronica Berger, Minneapolis, Minnesota*

> *I have a doll from days gone by— very worn and tattered. But she was there for me to love and that's all that really mattered.*
>
> —ANONYMOUS

CUTE AS A DOLL.
"Baby Peggy" (with me in the photo above) was my favorite doll in 1952. She had a cuddly cloth body, like a real baby. I remember the brown corduroy overalls I had on that day. Eventually, I got them for my dolls, too. I'd give anything to have that naturally curly hair back!

—*Cindy Walheim*
Parker, Pennsylvania

POPULAR PUPPET. Pop culture often gave rise to new toys. That was the case with Charlie McCarthy, the dummy of well-known ventriloquist Edgar Bergen. In 1940, when Sharon Spalding of Ashland, Oregon, had her photo taken for the Golden Spike Days celebration in Council Bluffs, Iowa, her Charlie McCarthy doll shared the spotlight.

DOUBLE THE PLEASURE.
"For our sixth birthdays, on July 26, 1947, Momma gave us a little party and our much-requested Betsy Wetsy dolls," remember Tennessee twins Catherine Hamilton Williams (left), now of Bluff City, and Virginia Hamilton Graves of Bristol. "Each doll came with only a shirt, diaper and bottle, but we were thrilled. It was not long after the war had ended and the dolls were not easily found, but Momma did. We really loved them!"

COWBOY WAS A STIFF.
"This 1937 picture shows me with the presents I received at my third birthday party," says JoAnn Cooke of Reseda, California. "Despite the fact that he had molded hair and a stiff, unbendable body, the cowboy doll quickly became a favorite. I remember crying a long time when he was lost a few years later."

Arlene and Virginia Ann

CONSTANT COMPANIONS. "I was given Raggedy Ann and Andy dolls at the age of 5, in 1947," says Virginia Butler, Milton, Pennsylvania. "Because I played with the dolls so much, Mom had a Christmas card made that year with the photo above. Reading the Raggedy Ann and Andy books by Johnny Gruelle a few years later really brought the dolls to life. What adventures they had!"

toys

TOYS HAVE THE POWER TO DEFINE A CHILDHOOD—AND AN ENTIRE GENERATION.

through the years

UNDERWOODARCHIVES.COM

TINKERING AROUND.
Tinkertoys have been inspiring budding engineers ever since their introduction around 1914. The construction sets were invented by Charles Pajeau of Evanston, Illinois, who saw children playing with sticks, pencils and empty spools of thread.

1920s

Perhaps the "Hopping '20s" would've suited this decade better. After all, it was then that American kids first caught on to the fad of the **pogo stick**. Although the pogo stick has never again been quite the rage that it was in the 1920s, it has, like many nostalgic toys, seen surges in popularity throughout the decades.

The die-cast car was another leading toy in the '20s. The mastermind behind these pocket-sized treasures was a company known as **TootsieToys**. Typically sold in small sets of a few cars or trucks, they were the precursor to Matchbox and Hot Wheels cars, popular in the 1950s, '60s and '70s.

Boys and girls spent hours building entire villages of log cabins thanks to **Lincoln Logs**. John Lloyd Wright, son of famous architect Frank Lloyd Wright, invented the construction toy in 1916, but it wasn't introduced to the public until several years later. Since then, more than 100 million sets have been sold.

1930s

While the toy industry didn't escape the effects of the Great Depression, those tough times became the inspiration behind many toys and games we still love today.

Board games ruled the decade. **Monopoly, Sorry!** and **Scrabble** were all invented in the 1930s. Although Scrabble didn't gain a larger following until the 1950s, Monopoly was an

instant success and has been one of the best-selling board games in the U.S. ever since.

Remember clicking your way through the slide frames of a favorite story on a **View-Master**? That toy made its debut at the 1939 New York World's Fair.

Speaking of pictures, a series of beloved movies led to one of the most coveted toys of the decade, the blue-eyed, golden-curled **Shirley Temple doll**.

1940s

The 1940s saw even more board games. **Candy Land** and **Chutes and Ladders** captured the attention of children, while **Clue** provided hours of family fun.

Cootie also entered the game scene in 1948. The object of this game was to be the first player to build a bug piece by piece from parts that included a body, a head, antennae, eyes and six legs. The game, which went on to sell millions, was the brainchild of letter carrier and inventor Herb Schaper.

The market for small toys boomed in the '40s, introducing such classics as **Silly Putty** and the **Slinky**. Like many inventions, Silly Putty came

MATCHBOX MEMORIES. Odette Landers of Fort Pierce, Florida, recalls that her son, Bruce, would spend hours playing with his toy cars. Not even Mom's camera could distract him!

BUSY BUILDERS. "I was three years older, but my brother, Greg, and I both enjoyed Lincoln Logs," says Douglas Clanin (in glasses), Anderson, Indiana.

about by accident, when engineers tried to make synthetic rubber. What they ended up with was a strange substance that bounced and stretched. Naval engineer Richard James developed the Slinky in the early 1940s. After a demonstration at Gimbels Department Store in Philadelphia in 1945, the store sold 400 Slinky toys in less than two hours.

Model airplanes and **Tonka trucks** found their way onto the wish lists of little boys everywhere during the '40s. Originally designed to help sell airplanes to the military, model airplanes became a hit. Tonka Toys, in their first year, produced a total of 37,000 metal trucks in two designs—a steam shovel and a crane. All were manufactured by the six-person staff of Mound Metalcraft Co., a garden tool business then located in a small schoolhouse basement in Mound, Minnesota.

1950s

Matchbox Cars, so named because of their size, zoomed onto the scene. The series became so popular that "Matchbox" was widely used by the public as a generic name for all pocket-size die-cast toy cars.

Mr. Potato Head became the first toy advertised on television. In the beginning, the toy consisted only of parts like the eyes, ears, nose, and mouth. It was up to the parents to provide the potato. Even so, this simple concept gained—and continues to enjoy—incredible success.

The **hula-hoop** and the '50s go hand in hand. The simple plastic hoop gained international popularity toward the end of the decade, even making its way into the lyrics of several popular songs of the time, including the 1958 Alvin and the Chipmunks song *Christmas Don't Be Late*.

The single toy that most would say defines the '50s is **Barbie**, introduced in 1959. Creator Ruth Handler envisioned a toy that would inspire girls to imagine what they might be as grown-ups, in the same way baby dolls encouraged them to care for children.

Over the decades, Barbie's popularity with little girls has only increased, as the onetime "teenage fashion model" has taken on many roles and professions.

1960s

Chatty Cathy was first released in stores and appeared in TV commercials beginning in 1960, and for her six-year run was the second in popularity only to Barbie. A doll ahead of her time, Chatty Cathy spoke one of 11 phrases, such as "I love you" or "Please take me with you," when the "chatty ring" on her back was pulled.

IVORY TICKLER. "My daughter, Patty, had just received this toy piano from her grandparents in 1957 for her second Christmas," Peggy Davis of Bishop, California, relates. "We lived in El Monte at the time. Sorry to say Patty did not continue playing the piano when she got older. But she sure had a lot of fun with that little one."

LOOK WHAT I GOT! "This slide is from Christmas Day of 1964 at our house in Dorchester, Massachusetts," notes Laura Thomas of Upton. "That's me on the left with my two older sisters, Nancy (middle) and Peggy, showing off our favorite presents received that year. I was so excited to receive my Pebbles doll Christmas morning. I remember that for my birthday, the following month, I got a Bamm-Bamm doll, too. I was a big fan of the prime-time show *The Flintstones*."

Television became a popular way to market new toys. In 1960 the Ohio Art Co. launched the **Etch A Sketch** and used TV to advertise the toy just in time for the holiday season.

TV also helped the sales of what would become the ultimate party game. **Twister** soared to success after Eva Gabor played it with Johnny Carson on the *Tonight Show* on May 3, 1966.

The **Easy-Bake Oven**, America's first working toy oven, was invented in 1963. Girls marveled at being able to bake just like Mom!

TONKA TITAN. "I took this picture of my son, Johnny, and his Tonka trucks at our home in Phoenix, Arizona, back in the '60s," reports Joan Backus from Prescott. Looks as if Johnny was ready to haul anything—cargo in the pickups, troops in the jeep and even more cars in the auto-hauler truck.

tikes&their trikes

BIKING BEAUTY. "I couldn't disguise my happiness when this 1941 photo was taken," says Myrna Johnson of Muskegon, Michigan. "Proudly sitting on my bike, complete with a bell, I'm all dolled up with a new dress from Mom and a head of cute curls!"

BIKE MAKER. "In 1945, bicycles were a scarcity because of the war," writes Jan Armentrout from Cedar Rapids, Iowa, "but our ingenious dad, who was a rural Watkins dealer, searched the countryside around Fayette and found two frames and two sets of handlebars. My sister Teressa (left) and I scraped off the rust and then painted the frames, hers red and mine blue. Dad ordered the other parts from Sears, Roebuck & Co. and assembled two sturdy bikes. Were we ever thrilled!"

1953

SECONDHAND WAS FIRST-RATE

"We didn't have a lot of money when I was growing up," says Louise LaMarca-Gay of Rochester, New Hampshire. "Most of our clothes were hand-me-downs from cousins. My cousin Priscilla had such pretty outfits that I felt privileged to have them. Sweets were rare, so we made the candy from Halloween last until the holidays.

"One Christmas was especially memorable. Dad picked up a bike and two tricycles from the dump and fixed them up for me (far left), my brother, Jimmy, and my sister, Elaine. He painted them, fixed the spokes, replaced the handlebar grips and put on new seat covers. To me, my present looked *brand new*. I didn't find out until years later the lengths Dad went to in order to make that day special for us. Yes, we were poor, but we had love, which was priceless."

toy cars put kids in the driver's seat

CHRISTMAS CAR.
"Shelby, Ohio, was feeling the early stages of the Depression in 1929," recalls Duane High, now of Tucson, Arizona. "But Dad was fortunate to be manager at a Standard Oil gas station, which allowed him to give me a pedal car for Christmas. It sure brought a smile to my 4-year-old face."

FOUR FOR THE DERBY. "My brothers and I each had a car in the 1938 Soap Box Derby in Bay City, Michigan, thanks to sponsors who paid for the wheels," says Richard Aeder of Akron, Michigan. "I'm second from left. At 9, I was barely old enough to race. My brother Rudy (left), at 15, was just under the age limit. Marvin (second from right) was 11, and Lester was 14. Marv and I raced for two more years. After the 1938 races, two of the cars were rebuilt into wagons that we used to peddle fruit, vegetables, smoked fish and Mom's homemade bread to help the family get through the Depression."

DRIVING PUTT-NIK

At the same time the Soviets were launching their Sputnik satellites into space, from 1957 to 1961, my dad was building a car that he named Putt-Nik.

My clever dad used the combustion engine from a Maytag washing machine and found a Ford Model T spark plug at an auto parts house.

Putt-Nik rolled on wagon wheels and wagon axles, the steering was a belt-and-pulley power train, the pads against the tires worked as brakes and Dad used a pulley slippage for the clutch. The body frame was constructed of two-by-fours, and the cowling was plywood.

When Dad stomped on the push crank in the back of the car with his foot, Putt-Nik responded with a loud "putt-putt-putt-putt!" The sound echoed through the neighborhood and, as if it were a Pied Piper's flute, drew kids hoping for a ride.

—*Janice Simcoe, Fair Oaks, California*

MY FIRST CAR. "I was 3 in 1927 and driving my 'Buick' when this photo was taken in Wausau, Wisconsin," relates Jean Gappa. "My parents couldn't figure out where I picked up the name 'Buick.' They didn't know anyone who owned one, and there certainly was no TV advertising in those days. But it was *my* Buick and no one tried to convince me it wasn't."

A MEAN MACHINE. "Using a gasoline engine from a washing machine, my uncle Fulton built a toy car for me in 1935," says Richard Downing, Fort Myers, Florida. "I cranked the foot pedal to start it up and pushed a gearshift handle forward to tighten a belt, which steered the rear axle. There was only one forward gear and only one speed. The brakes were manual—I had to put my feet in a hole in the floorboard and drag them on the ground!" In this photo, Richard is driving his neighbor, James Clements, in the annual firemen's parade in Milford, Delaware. His uncle borrowed a siren from the firemen and mounted it on the hood of the car.

lionel trains were a treasured tradition

By Thomas Gore Jr., Kennett Square, Pennsylvania

Lionel trains were a big part of every Christmas for my family when I was growing up in Philadelphia. Weeks before, my four brothers and I would run over to the hobby store to pick up a copy of the latest Lionel catalog. Back at home, we'd feverishly circle all the new trains and equipment we wanted and then carefully place the catalog under Dad's pillow.

My brothers and I would look high and low in all the closets to get a sneak peek at our presents before Mom and Dad put them under the tree. We never had any luck, and to this day I don't know where they hid them.

But the real magic came on Christmas morning. My parents would wait until we kids were in bed on Christmas Eve before decorating the tree and setting up the platform for the trains. It was always so exciting to wake up and see those trains running on the track! My brothers and I didn't even mind too much that we were not allowed to open gifts until after Mass.

While we never got everything we greedily circled in that catalog, Mom and Dad would usually surprise us with a new piece to add to the train collection, which the whole family treasured.

TRAINED TO BE PATIENT. For Thomas Gore (shown here at age 5, in 1948) and his brothers, Christmas meant new cowboy gear and another addition to their Lionel train collection. But gift opening had to wait until after Mass.

A ONE-TRACK MIND !

When it comes to trains, boys have a one-track mind.
They want Lionel Trains . . . nothing else is the real thing. They
know that only Lionel has *Magne-Traction.**
They know that nothing else approaches the true-to-life realism
of Lionel's scale detailing. You can't fool today's youngsters . . .
and for solid value, it's better not to try. Just follow
his "one-track mind" to your Lionel dealer's!

*The permanent power-plus that means . . .
More Speed! More Pull! More Climb! More Control!*

LIONEL TRAINS

Stop in at your Lionel dealer's for   the great new 40-page Lionel Trains catalog

1953

the die was cast

LEAD SOLDIERS CAPTURED HIS CURIOSITY IN 1936 AND NEVER LET GO.

By Ralph Gauvey, Fort Myers, Florida

Homemade lead soldiers have always held a fascination for me. When I was in the sixth grade, in 1936, I talked my parents into buying me a kit to make the lead soldiers at our home in Dayton, Ohio.

The kit contained a ladle, a few small bars of lead, an instruction book and three forms to make World War I soldiers—one marching, one shooting, and the largest one, an officer on a horse.

Getting more lead, however, was a problem. Luckily, there was a monument factory just a short way up the alley from my house. It was small and old-fashioned, with machinery powered by one engine and belts running in every direction.

Outside were slabs of granite of all sizes, and each one contained four or more holes that were filled with lead.

I believe that when the slabs were shipped, steel bolts were put in the holes and lead was poured in to secure the bolts so that the granite could be lifted.

Those pieces of granite were my lead mine, providing raw material for my soldiers.

Getting the lead out wasn't easy. You needed a hammer and chisel or, since my dad didn't have a chisel, a large screwdriver. I think I ruined three or more of his screwdrivers—he'd stand there and stare at them, wondering what had happened. I just observed innocently. But those screwdrivers and my sweat provided me with a veritable army of lead soldiers.

I had only the three molds, but other boys had different molds and we traded soldiers. And once I traded a few for a paddleball toy.

My mom was very supportive of my making lead soldiers. She warned me to be careful and was sometimes in the kitchen when I melted the lead in the ladle—a couple of tablespoons, perhaps—to make one soldier at a time.

"Mind you, don't spill any of that on the linoleum," she'd say.

I suspected that if I ever did spill any, there was a chance of burning down the house. I was always careful.

I have three of those soldiers on my desk now and sometimes wonder what happened to all the rest that I had so much fun making and trading.

Ironically, they all seem to have melted away again!

the cowboy craze

EVERY LITTLE BOY DREAMED OF HOPPING ON HIS HORSE AND HEADING OUT TO FIGHT BANDITS.

RANGER AT THE READY. Four-year-old Roger Cox couldn't be coaxed to bed without his cowboy hat and toy guns at his side. Says his mother, Barbara Cox, of Oldsmar, Florida, "He always slept with them in case he needed them in a hurry!"

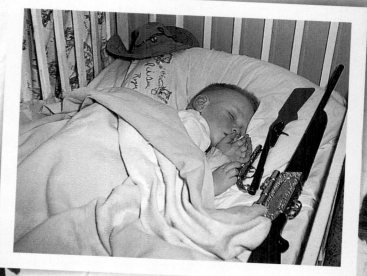

HOWDY, COWBOY. "I keep this picture of my late husband, Robert, in my wallet," writes Linda Rakich of Niles, Ohio. "The story goes that when he was 6 years old, in 1952, the teacher told the students they could bring in their favorite toy for show and tell. Robert happily took a toy gun and holster that his uncle had bought for him. But when Robert continued to come to school with the toys for the rest of the week, the teacher finally had to tell him to leave them at home!"

KING ME. "The slides we took in the '50s are so special to us because they were the first color pictures we had," relates Lillian Patterson of Lansing, Michigan. "The favorite is this one of our sons Kern and Ray playing checkers on the game board they got for Christmas. Our son Leland, who was 17 at the time, took the picture." The game board also could be used for backgammon.

GIFTS KNOCKED THEM OUT!

The Christmas of 1957 was a happy one for the Patterson clan living in Albuquerque, New Mexico. "For some reason, I had been hitting things around the house all year," says Daniel Patterson, now of Keene, New Hampshire. "My parents must have thought the punching bag was a good way to channel my energy! I was eager to try it out with Dad.

"My sister, Bobbie, had asked for a nurse doll that year. You can tell from the way she's gazing at it in this photo that she couldn't have been happier. Coincidentally, she went on to become a nurse, just like Mom."

LET'S PLAY "PAPES."

"In the 1940s, playing with paper dolls—or 'papes'—was a favorite pastime for my sister, Lynne, and me (on left)," recalls Joy Sander, Warminster, Pennsylvania. "As we carefully punched the dolls and clothes out of the books, it was important to avoid cutting off a vital tab that helped hold the clothing in place. To enhance our collection, we cut out models and clothes from the Sears, Roebuck catalog."

Growing Up

it's in the bag!

Remember shooting for aggies, steelies and cat's-eyes
in a game of ringer? Royce Lain sure had a determined look in
this slide taken by Bob Taylor from Cordell, Oklahoma, about 1952.
Bob says the game took place on the Lain farm east of Rocky,
where Sylvia and Charles "Cheesy" Lain were wheat farmers.

CHAPTER SEVEN

School Days

From riding the bus and eating in the cafeteria to doing homework and going to assemblies, school marked the first time we ventured off to chart our own course. Yes, school days were always an adventure!

"The first day of school was often more important to our mothers than it was to us children during World War II," says Pat Brown (below) of Redington Shores, Florida. "Because money was an issue, returning to school often meant wearing last year's clothes. This could be downright embarrassing after an active growing season, when outgrown dresses barely covered your new underwear.

"Limited supplies also meant getting sturdy brown shoes, not Mary Janes or saddle shoes. Yet another thing my mother thought necessary before opening day was a Toni home permanent!

"Looking back, I can smile at the clothes and the way we looked, because in every picture, we were carrying books. And that was the whole point."

Turn the page for more stories from the dear old Golden Rule days...

when our team 'went to state'

By Beverly Olthoff Knebel
Greenfield, Wisconsin

Thinking back to my high school years, I still recall the excitement I felt in 1940 when our girls' basketball team made it to the state tournament.

My hometown of Kamrar, population 250, was in Iowa's corn belt. About the only thing to do there was play basketball! Though I lived in town, most of my teammates were farmers' daughters.

We trained hard to win. Our handsome young coach had us run daily on the country roads outside of town. (Most of us had a crush on him, so we would have followed him anywhere!)

We had to win a lot of playoff games to get to the state tournament—first the county, then the sectional, then the district. All that travel was heady stuff for us.

During the sectional tournament, we stayed overnight in a nice private home with an *indoor* bathroom. (My family had an outdoor privy.) I awoke before everyone else and took a bath—what luxury for a girl used to a galvanized washtub next to the kitchen stove on Saturday night!

Basketball was so big in our little community that when our team reached the state tournament, the whole town closed down. The only restaurant locked its doors, and most homes were empty as everyone traveled to Drake University in Des Moines to watch the action.

We girls got to stay in the immense Hotel Savery, with its classy rooms and crisp white linens on the beds. (At home, we had flannel sheets.)

At night, we girls had a big time running from room to room, giggling and screaming. Finally, a man in one of the adjoining rooms sent a bellboy to our door with a box of candy bars and a plea to "tone it down a little."

We were just having fun and hadn't thought of other people trying to sleep. After that, keeping the noise level down was

CHOCOLATE-COVERED BRIBE. Beverly Knebel (first row, second from left) and her teammates were given a sweet incentive to keep the noise down at their high-class hotel.

KAMRAR, H.S. SQUAD 1939-40

JAMES PHOTO

a true test of will, but this just added to the adventure. (I still have the wrapper from that late-night candy "bribe.")

Breakfast in the elegant hotel restaurant was dazzling, with waiters, white tablecloths and napkins. I felt like a princess digging a shiny spoon into my first grapefruit. (I really didn't like it, but I wouldn't admit that.)

Later, as we walked the streets of Des Moines proudly wearing our team jackets, we were treated like celebrities. I felt great in my black skirt, red sweater, long pearls tied in a knot and bobby socks with saddle shoes.

Evaded an Interview
That afternoon, a reporter from the Oskaloosa paper sent a note to the hotel room asking to meet me for an interview. I misunderstood his note, thinking he was asking me for a date. I refused to meet him!

All this attention was flattering, but I was just a team player. My cousin Liz was the real star, later named All-American. Our coach always told us to "feed the ball to Liz."

Sadly, we ended up losing the state tourney by one point. Oh, how hard we played and how bitter the defeat!

I'm a grandmother now, and my athletic days are long over. But I'll always have those glory years…along with a crumbling booklet filled with old news clippings and a candy bar wrapper. Someone seeing me leafing through the yellowed pages of my scrapbook might think, *She has only memories left*. But I'm still that giggling girl inside, and I always will be. So, how about it…anyone for an autograph?

after-school snack
The age of 16 was certainly sweet for Sally Lucas (wearing the scarf in this 1946 photo). "When school let out one April afternoon, my friend Bobby Walker (in the driver's seat) took a bunch of us for a drive in her convertible," remembers Sally, of Roanoke, Virginia. "We stopped at the local Dairy Fountain for a treat. We thought we were hot stuff!"

BACK TO SCHOOL.
These two boys seem to be taking their time, which means they were probably going to school rather than coming home. They wouldn't have believed it at the time, but those school days were destined to produce some great memories.

A+ class pictures

STILL CHUMS TODAY.

"Sister Antonina was my teacher at Our Lady of Lourdes in Brooklyn, New York," says Angela Beetz of Springhill, Florida. "There were 64 kids in our class of 1953. The room was actually double the size of what you see here. I'm in the third row, second from the right. Gabriella 'Ella' Vellani is the third girl to my right. Ella and I are on the phone twice a month and see each other at least once a year."

BIRDS OF A FEATHER.

"As a kindergartner at Franklin School in Wichita, Kansas, in 1930, we made birdhouses as a class project. I'm the girl in the front row with my hand on my face," says June Kennedy from Phoenix. "The effects of the Depression were all around us, but we found simple ways to have fun."

HER ROLE MODEL.

"This 1924 picture is of my first-grade class at Warren School in Decatur, Illinois," writes Mary Smith of Long Beach, California. "I'm second from the left in the first row and my brother, Paul White, is second from the left in the second row. The teacher was Miss Pearson, whom I dearly loved. My mother said I talked so much about her that she got a little tired of hearing the name. I had already determined I would be a teacher."

WE BANDED TOGETHER.

"At our elementary school in Houma, Louisiana, students were assigned to classrooms alphabetically by last name," shares Herman Domangue of Colorado Springs, Colorado. "The only exceptions were the members of the band. Every year we were in the same classes, lunch period and recess.

"The photo at right was taken in 1955, a memorable year for the group. Only four bands received a 'superior' rating at the state competition—and we were one of them." Herman is on the far right in the third row.

THE STUDIOUS TYPES. "This picture, taken in 1936, shows my second-grade class at Myra Bradwell School on the south side of Chicago," explains Marilyn Blake Vander Geest of Marshall, Michigan. "I'm fourth from the right in the back row. When I got to high school, I was able to skip the typing class because of what I learned in the second grade.

"I eventually became an elementary school secretary, a job I held for 25 years. My boss once showed this photograph to the school board to assure them that it was possible for students to learn to type at a young age. I'm living proof."

lessons in helping others

MILKWEED WAR EFFORT.
"During World War II, country schools throughout Iowa collected milkweed pods so the silks could be used to make parachutes and life jackets," writes Edna Small of Mount Ayr. "In 1944, I was attending Otter Creek School, which was a runner-up in the state for collecting 130 sacks of the pods." The top photo at left shows the stuffed sacks hanging on the fence around the schoolyard.

"It took several days to gather the pods, but we enjoyed getting out of schoolwork for a few hours each day," Edna says. "As the only girl in Mrs. Plumb's class, I had to be a tomboy to keep up with the others!"

NO KIDDING AROUND.
Older students often served as crossing guards to help kids get home safely. Here a boy takes his job seriously, holding his sign up high so that the children stay safe on the sidewalk until he gives the OK to venture into the street.

STOP

> *It is hard to convince a high school student that he will encounter a lot of problems more difficult than those of algebra and geometry.*
>
> —EDGAR W. HOWE

THEY ALSO SERVED. Michigan elementary schoolboys, including the author (front row, right), knitted afghan squares to help out in World War II.

knitting for victory

These children joined squares and purled their efforts to help on the home front in 1943.

By Richard Mathewson, Norman, Oklahoma

During World War II, everyone in Owosso, Michigan, was involved on the home front, even grade-school kids like me who were asked to knit afghans for the wounded veterans.

All of us had relatives in the service and realized we were part of the war effort. I was 10 years old in 1943 and really enjoyed the knitting. I think I did it for a while before I drifted on to other things.

This photograph (above) appeared in the *Owosso Argus Press* along with an article about our efforts at Emerson Elementary School in my hometown, west of Flint.

Because of the labor shortage, my mother was working at the newspaper. Another man at the paper who had a student at the school thought our project was worth reporting—people were always interested in what the children were doing to help.

The story noted that 30 of the 45 boys in the fourth through sixth grades had made at least one square as a Junior Red Cross project.

"The boys are really very patient and are willing to do the squares over and over again to get them right," one teacher said in the story. "My son has had to rip one of his out four times.

"It is a lot to expect that youngsters in the fourth grade turn in perfect knitting, but we do get some fine pieces of work," another fourth-grade teacher said.

We did the knitting after our lessons were done or took the work home to do.

"My pupils can knit better than I can," one teacher remarked. "There's not a single thing these youngsters of mine can't do."

The afghan that we worked on actually went to a wounded veteran who was a relative of one of the kids in the school. That made our handiwork even more rewarding.

SEW FOR SCHOOL DAYS

Hair all shining, faces all scrubbed...and, bright as flying autumn leaves, Bates crisp combed cottons for first-day-of-school. They're in clear crayon colors, *very* little-girl, vat-dyed and Sanforized*, to sew to Simplicity Printed Patterns 1851 (bolero) and 2096. BATES FABRICS, INC., 80 WORTH STREET, NEW YORK 13

*Residual shrinkage less than 1%

Bates FABRICS

dress-up day had storybook ending

By Joan Calder, Plantation, Florida

The first day of school brought a buzz of excitement to the children attending Clarkesville Elementary School in Georgia. The most important question was, "What teacher did you get?" No one wanted the mean or strict teacher, or the one who gave a lot of homework. But most important, we wanted to be in the same class as our best friends.

Fourth grade, which I entered in 1961, turned out to be lucky for me. Not only were my best friends and I in the same class, but we were assigned to Mrs. Lovell, a wonderful teacher who made education fun—and who never gave homework over the weekend.

One day, Mrs. Lovell announced that we were to come to school dressed as our favorite storybook character. The special day was several weeks away, and somehow I forgot to tell my mother about it. The big day arrived, and I woke up in a panic with no costume to wear. To make things worse, my mother had already left for the day.

My aunt Brenda was baby-sitting us five kids, getting everyone up and off to school. When I finally worked up the nerve to break the news, my kindhearted aunt helped me dress up as Heidi. She quickly rounded up a vest, an apron and a ribbon to tie around my neck, and I happily headed off to school.

I didn't care that my friend outshone me in her handmade Heidi costume. My heart was filled with gratitude for Aunt Brenda, who saved me from an embarrassing day.

beyond the books

SCHOOL PLAYS, BAND CONCERTS AND OTHER PERFORMANCES WERE OFTEN PART OF THE CURRICULUM.

FOREFATHERS AND FOREMOTHERS. Well, back in 1922, they were still just eight kids when this Washington's Birthday pageant was put on by the second-graders at McAlister School in Lawrence, Kansas. James Burdette Smith of Kansas City, Missouri, sent in the patriotic photo. That's James at far left in the back row.

LET IT SNOW FOR THE SHOW. "In 1937, the grammar school children in San Leandro, California, performed at the Oakland Auditorium," says Elaine Tasoulas, Ridgefield, Washington. "Every school had a weather theme. As you can tell by the giant 'snowballs' we're holding, our sixth-grade class danced to a winter theme." In the photo below, Elaine is in the front row on the far right.

TALENTED TWIRLERS. "I was part of the twirling squad at Bisbee High School in Arizona in 1942," remembers Martha Tolbert of Tucson. "There was a globe at one end of the baton that could light up. When they turned off the lights at the park or football field, we would turn on our batons and create a formation, which drew oohs and aahs from the crowd. In the photo here, I'm in the top row on the far left."

VOILÀ, THE VIOLA!
"In 1926, I was a 12-year-old budding musician with the junior orchestra at Mark Twain School in Webster Groves, Missouri," writes Ione Pinsker of Fortuna, California (second row, right of the triangle).
"By the time they got to me, the only remaining instrument was the viola, which I disliked, but I had promised to finish the semester on any available instrument. My real education was learning to appreciate music and recognize and enjoy accomplished musicians."

fun in the cafeteria

COLD LUNCH OR HOT, BROWN BAG OR LUNCH BOX,
NOONTIME WAS MEMORABLE.

Good to the Last Crumb

Our cafeteria in Erie, Kansas, had to provide well-balanced lunches, as many of the kids from the country were bused to the consolidated school and had to eat there.

When I was in the eighth grade in 1951, I was selected to take the money from the high school students as they came in for lunch.

The lunch always included dessert and often it was chocolate cake. The cooks found out I loved chocolate cake and began saving an extra piece for me. They even left the baking pans so I could eat the cake crumbs and frosting that stuck to the sides.

The cooks continued to do this for me until I graduated in 1956, as I always ate lunch in the school cafeteria.

I have fond memories of those cooks—and that chocolate cake. I don't think I've eaten any that good since.

—*Barbara Harvey, Dallas, Texas*

Too Cool for Lunch Box

My father, Donald Jorgensen, took the photo above in May of 1956. It was just before my friends and I graduated from Washington High School in Sioux Falls, South Dakota, where Dad was a biology teacher.

I am wearing a striped blouse, sitting across the table from Lois Engen Bahnson in the white blouse and purple skirt.

Most of the students who didn't eat the cafeteria food carried their lunches in brown paper bags. Carrying a lunch box was not cool.

—*Patricia Jorgensen Palagi*
Seattle, Washington

Growing Up

bus driver eased his fears

By Bruce Squiers, Salem, New York

Even by the relatively low standards of the postwar era, it wasn't much of a bus, but I'll always remember Bus 11.

I was a kindergartner with limited social skills living in Cambridge, New York, in 1954. The bus driver, Mr. Hamilton, was a friendly, caring man with children of his own. His empathy is what made me remember Bus 11.

One day en route home, I got crammed into the back of the bus and, when it reached my stop, I couldn't get out. As the bus emptied, I took the nearest available seat and froze. Was I destined to spend the rest of my life on this bus?

The bus continued its run, and Mr. Hamilton saw me and realized that I should have departed long before. He quickly sensed my predicament.

"Don't worry. I'll make sure you get home all right," he said. He moved me to the seat directly behind him and tried to make me comfortable.

Mr. Hamilton figured out my name, told me stories to keep my mind occupied and explained that he'd get me back to my house when he had completed his run.

As my parents were beginning to worry about my whereabouts, Bus 11 pulled into their driveway and I was personally escorted to my house by Mr. Hamilton.

I doubt if he ever really remembered the incident, but it made a big impression on me.

To this day, I can't recall half the buses I ever rode on, although I can always see Bus 11 in my mind.

I often think the world would be a more joyous place if it had more Mr. Hamiltons.

favorite old-time poem

"I heard this poem often while attending school," writes Cindi Kiser of Oklahoma City. "It always left me with the image of letters dressed up in pinafores and sailor suits, trooping into a one-room schoolhouse under the direction of a stern-faced schoolmarm!"

The Letters at School

By Mary Mapes Dodge

One day the letters went to school,
And tried to learn each other;
They got so mixed 'twas really hard
To pick out one from t'other.

A went in first, and Z went last;
The rest all were between them,
K, L and M, and N, O, P,
I wish you could have seen them!

Now, through it all the Consonants
Were rudest and uncouthest,
While all the pretty Vowel girls
Were certainly the smoothest.

And simple U kept far from Q,
With face demure and moral,
"Because," she said, "we are, we two,
So apt to start a quarrel!"

But spiteful P said, "Pooh for U!"
(Which made her feel quite bitter),
And calling O, L, E to help,
He really tried to hit her.

Meanwhile, when U and P made up,
The Cons'nants looked about them,
And kissed the Vowels, for, you see,
They could not do without them.

it's signed!

Lee Turner Jr. is smiling because he just brought home his first report card, and Dad signed it. His father, now of Norwood, New York, says, "The slide is from about 1960, when we lived in Norfolk, New York. Lee Jr. brought home a lot more report cards over the years, and I signed them all. He was a very bright boy."

school's out! school's out!

Remember the bell ringing to signal the end
of the school year—and the start of summer vacation?
The faces of the schoolchildren in this photo are filled
with pure joy—they know they have several months of fun
in the sun. No more pencils, no more books,
no more teachers' dirty looks!

School Days

164

CHAPTER EIGHT

Family Album

Nothing tells the story of our growing-up years quite like a captivating selection of snapshots. Sometimes the expressions on our faces say more about our emotions than words ever could.

"In the photo below, it's pretty clear that I idolized my dad," says Chuck Beers of Hollister, Missouri. "The 1947 picture—with me wearing Dad's policeman's hat and brandishing a cap pistol—was taken when a Des Moines, Iowa, newspaper ran a series of articles on public servants who worked odd shifts and how they stayed in touch with their children.

"Dad kept in touch with my brother, sister and me by occasionally taking one of us to work with him. Once in a while, we'd get to ride in a patrol car.

"At the time of the article, Dad had been assigned to duty inside police headquarters after being injured as a motorcycle officer. I'd often join him on his 4-p.m.-to-midnight shift and sleep on a piece of plywood that Dad placed atop the steam radiator. It was flat and hard, but warm. You can bet I was always proud to say my dad was a policeman!"

Sit back, relax and take a photographic journey down memory lane.

◀ My mother made a beautiful little dress and took me to a photo studio for this portrait in 1928, when I was 18 months old. The photographer handed me the doll in an effort to make me smile, but his plan didn't work. I was sad when he tried to take the doll away, thus the pout.

—*Gene Marsh*
Knoxville, Tennessee

▶ When I was a child in the '30s, few families owned cameras, so they depended on traveling photographers. The day one came to our area, Mom and Dad wanted a photo of me on our front porch so badly that they had him take this shot of me—mumps and all!

—*Doris Belovich, Parma, Ohio*

I fell under the spell of a photo booth at Woolworth's as a Thomas Carr Howe High School freshman in Irvington, Indiana, back in 1942. If the hairdo was not bad enough, my facial expression progressed from a sultry Lauren Bacall wannabe to a wild-eyed Phyllis Diller. At the time, I fantasized about being in the movies someday, and when the flashbulbs in the booth went off, I became a star!

—*Jo Justice Stewart*
Solon Springs, Wisconsin

In 1955, our dancing class performed the story of Cinderella. My sister Jo Ann (wearing the top hat) played Prince Charming, because she'd cracked a bone in her foot and couldn't toe-dance with the rest of us. I'm on the left. Mom always made the wonderful costumes for all of our performances.

—*Mary Ann Gove*
Cottonwood, Arizona

On a hot July day in 1943, my family moved from New York to Connecticut. My sister, Nancy, and I were suddenly two city kids stranded in the country. One morning we awoke to discover Dad had set up this hammock between two shady trees in our yard. Nancy and I enjoyed it all summer long and became not only closer sisters, but best friends as well.

—*Lorelei Gelzer, Redmond, Washington*

▲ Royce (left) and Gerald Lain look to be devouring the booty from a watermelon raid in this photo captured by Bob Taylor, of Cordell, Oklahoma, for his business, Agricultural Photos, in the early 1950s. They were on the Lain farm, east of Rocky, Oklahoma, where the boys' parents, Sylvia and Charles "Cheesie" Lain, raised wheat. Doesn't this picture just make you want to dive into a melon and let that sweet juice run down your chin?

There were 15 boys living on our small neighborhood block. We never lacked for players in our football, baseball and basketball games. Many times the games would end in fights, but by the next day all was forgiven and we were ready to play again. In this 1950 photo, I'm on the far right.

—*David King, Greenville, Ohio*

The summer of 1968 was one of the best of my childhood, because it was the year I learned to play baseball. The yards in our Chicago neighborhood were small—and our landlord didn't want any broken windows—so the games took place in the alley. I was only 6 (I'm at far right), but it didn't matter: All the neighbor kids played together, despite our age differences.

—*Bryan Barber, Boise, Idaho*

Visiting my grandparents was always a treat, especially on Christmas, when most of us kids wore an outfit from Santa. As you can tell from their attire, my cousins Mike and Melinda Price were big fans of Roy Rogers and Dale Evans in 1958. I'm the second from the right, showing off a spiffy sweater.

—*Paul Prough*
Mount Union, Pennsylvania

▲ During World War II, this lot on Van Wart Avenue in White Plains, New York, where we played football and softball, was used for victory gardens. In this December 1951 photo, I'm in the center of the back row. Richie Garifano (front row, far right) was the only one of us to play high school football. He was voted an all-county player.

—*George Edmundson, Keller, Texas*

◄

Mom would often take my brother and me to a park near our Albany, New York, home. During the summer of 1960, a man approached my mom and asked to take a picture of us playing cops and robbers. This photo, with me in the dark shorts, was taken by award-winning photographer Martin Miller and appeared in a publication for photographers. I cherish this moment frozen in time.

—*James Burns*
Richmond, Virginia

This photo was taken on a Boy Scout camping trip in Wading River, New York, in 1948. Two years earlier, I'd received my Webelos badge from Cub Scout Troop 128. It was a big day for me!

—*John Hemmer*
New York, New York

The headline in the *Jamestown Post-Journal*, Jamestown, New York, told the story on this day in August 1945. My brothers, Larry, 8 (right), and Roger, 2 (center), and a neighborhood friend, Roger Hager, dressed up to celebrate the end of World War II. Those who served were heroes to us.

—*Celeste Kerns*
Westfield, New York

▲ In this photo from the 1920s in Grand Forks, North Dakota, our little brother Tom targeted my sister and me with a refreshing summer spray. I'm the one getting the full force of the hose. Sister Kay and I are sporting our older sisters' swimsuits, as you can tell from how I have my suit hitched up at the shoulders. Wearing hand-me-downs did not dampen our spirit of fun, though.

—*Jo Bach, Fargo, North Dakota*

► The young entrepreneurs in this lemonade business are (from left) Ray Weliky, Ray Schneck, Max Andrae and Dick Andrae in a 1928 photograph.

▲ This photo was taken at Christmas 1959 while my family was living in Lewiston, New York. I had just received a doctor's kit and decided my cousin, Martin Zess, was the perfect patient.

—*Bonnie Walker-Legere*
West Palm Beach, Florida

►

We often took our eldest son, Dale, to swing at the park. As you can see, he loved it. This slide was taken in 1948 at a park located on the east side of Pueblo, Colorado, where we were living at the time.

—*Mary Heberly, Canon City, Colorado*

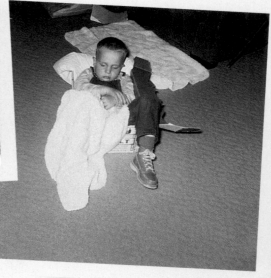

▲ I'm pictured here with our family's cocker spaniel, Chip, on Big Star Lake near Baldwin, Michigan, in 1948. Although our family had five dogs during my youth, Chip was my favorite. When not wading and chasing minnows at our cottage, he'd hunt for mice in the outfield as I played baseball with friends back home.

—*Jack Laansma, Mount Prospect, Illinois*

▲ Playing hard can really tucker a kid out! Our son, Paul, was about 5 when I snapped this photo. He had been playing with a cardboard box and decided it made a nice little bed for a nap.

—*Betty O'Briant, Hinton, Ohio*

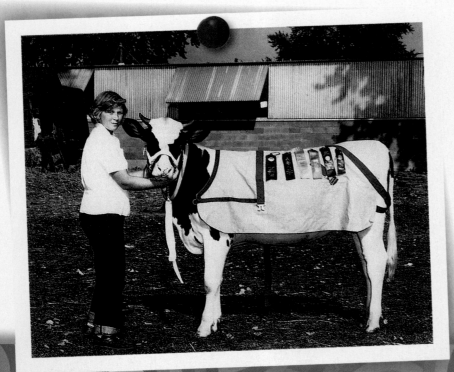

◀
At age 8, I followed my father's example and joined 4-H. I learned early how to pick winning calves for the show ring and won many awards through the years. When I was 17, my senior yearling, Andrea, placed first at the 1955 Ohio State Fair. Up next was the local fair, which turned out to be one of the hottest recorded. Andrea was a trouper, but on her fifth trip to the show ring, she had enough of the oppressive heat and lay down. The gallery roared. Eventually, Andrea got up to claim the blanket and white halter she's wearing in this photo.

—*Carol Eyster, Wetumka, Oklahoma*

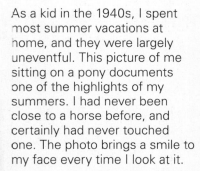

As a kid in the 1940s, I spent most summer vacations at home, and they were largely uneventful. This picture of me sitting on a pony documents one of the highlights of my summers. I had never been close to a horse before, and certainly had never touched one. The photo brings a smile to my face every time I look at it.

—*Dom Guarneri*
Naples, Florida

When there was work to be done around the house, we were eager to jump in and be Dad's right-hand man. Apart from an occasional outburst of frustration, he patiently taught us the handyman skills we put to work later in life.

J.C. ALLEN AND SON

▲ My dad, an avid photographer, took this photo of my cousin Ginger (right) and me in the summer of 1958. We were enjoying Popsicles from the ice cream truck that had just gone by my house in Rockford. Ginger and I spent a lot of time together as kids, so this photo brings back many pleasant memories.
    —*Lori Zagorski, Rockford, Illinois*

When my sister, Elaine, and I got into our mom's lipstick one day in 1949, Dad was there to capture the moment. Elaine is the serious one. We lived in Hurricane, Utah, at the time. Dad liked to take pictures and always had his camera ready.

—*Leilani Davis, Cedar City, Utah*

My daughter Roxie was trying her hand at making a pie crust in this slide from 1966. She was in the kitchen at our house in Adams County, Pennsylvania. Looks like a sticky rolling pin is giving her some troubles!

—*Joan C. Kump, Aspers, Pennsylvania*

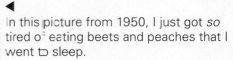

In this picture from 1950, I just got *so* tired of eating beets and peaches that I went to sleep.

—*Valerie Timm Adams*
Spokane, Washington

▲ In the summer of 1941, my aunt, Bertha Snyder, took me to Atlantic City, New Jersey, to give my mother, who was expecting my brother, a break. After two weeks, we ran out of money. Our supper the night before this picture was taken was bologna and bread in our room. But the next morning, money from home arrived, and we were walking down the street planning what to order for breakfast when a roving photographer snapped our picture.

—*Barbara Kernaghan, Davenport, Florida*

▲ My daughter, Karen, may be only 3 years old in this 1963 photo, but she has to squat to be at eye level with a pygmy goat at Fantasy Island amusement park in Niagara Falls, New York.

—*Bill Young, Oneida, New York*

◄ While on a trip out west, my daughter Gayle found the path to Washington's Mount Rainier a little tiring. She decided this big boulder was the perfect place to rest before continuing with the climb.

—*Noreen Collier
Jackson, Michigan*

When the "Paper Troopers" hit the streets of New Orleans in 1945, we collected some 700 pounds of paper a day. The papers were taken to the fire station for recycling, and the money was used for firemen's pensions, a station wagon for the city's neighborhood center and recreational equipment for the troops on occupation duty in the Pacific. We received a certificate of merit, and a party for all the Troopers was held the summer of 1946. In this photo, taken by my aunt, I'm in the striped shirt showing off an old issue of *Life* magazine to my brother, Robert.

—*Eugene Cresson*
New Orleans, Louisiana

I worked for the Chicago Public Library and its book caravan during the summers of my high school and college years. The best part was seeing the children waiting for us to arrive at our different locations each day. The experience led me to a lifelong career in teaching. Seated at the table in this 1955 photo, I'm on the right.

—*Barbara Deichmann*
Lake Forest, California

▲ Dating for teenagers in the 1950s often involved a stop at the local diner for a milk shake. When things between a couple got serious, they'd order one drink and two straws.

▼ My dad and uncle purchased a country grocery store in 1919, the year I was born. I had many jobs there as I got older, including stocking the shelves and operating the switchboard. (The store also served as a small local telephone company.) When this photo was taken in 1929, I was sitting down to enjoy a candy bar while Mom served two customers. My brother bought the store in 1937 and ran it until the early 1950s.

—*Lawrence Scharine*
Delavan, Wisconsin

▲ The boy in this photo likely heard the music of the ice cream truck from blocks away and hurried to ask Mom for a few coins so he could buy a cool, creamy treat. Remember the disappointment when the truck disappeared down the street before you had a chance to stop it?

◄

Before teenagers started gathering with friends at shopping malls, they'd head over to the local drive-in restaurant to meet up with their pals for some cheap eats—hamburgers, fries, soda pop, milk shakes. The menu has pretty much stayed the same from generation to generation.

▲ Kids didn't need a special trip to the store to buy kites. With paper, a little paint and a few strings, they could make their own. The fun continued when you ran full speed ahead in hopes the kite would catch some wind and you could send it soaring into the sky.

◄

Heads turned when I drove my 1927 Model T around town or past the high school in Penne Grove, New Jersey, in 1932. That's me behind the wheel. One time, my friend and I painted the car our school colors of red and white—with house paint!

—Don Willis
Cherry Hill, New Jersey

lap of luxury

This is my most cherished picture. That's me at age 3, just before Christmas of 1947. We lived with my grandparents Joseph and Alfretta Wheller in Paxtang, Pennsylvania. Whenever I asked, "Grandpa, please hold me," he would pull me onto his lap and read to me. Here he is reading from my favorite storybook, *The Night Before Christmas*. It would later be the first book I learned to read. I think this is such a sweet moment. I treasure this picture and the memories of my grandpa.

—*Bonnie Bair, Manchester, Maryland*

CHAPTER NINE

Holidays & Celebrations

Valentine's Day...Easter...Halloween...Thanksgiving...Christmas...birthdays.
Gatherings with friends and family throughout the year promised all sorts of
fun and excitement for kids. No matter the season, there was always a reason
to celebrate.

"In 1945, when my husband, Donald Naylor (standing third from right in
photo below right), was in kindergarten in Owatonna, Minnesota, the maypole
signaled the arrival of spring," writes Jerrilin Naylor, La Grange, Kentucky.

"May 1 was the day to form a circle around
the pole, which had been decorated with
colored streamers made from crepe paper.
Taking turns, each child would scurry and set a
small basket of candy behind a classmate.

"Then all the children would peek behind
themselves to see if the basket was there. If
it was, the student would take off running to
catch the classmate who left it and give the
child a big hug."

Relive such carefree occasions again by
turning the page.

my grandest birthday party

By Norman Smith
Tampa, Florida

I've had many great birthdays, but the memory of my sixth birthday in 1942 really takes me back to a peaceful time when we never locked our doors and we only closed the windows during a blowing rainstorm.

What a party that was. No—we didn't go to a pricey pizza place with lots of video games, like kids do today. Instead, it was a small gathering of my best friends.

First we enjoyed games like hide-and-seek and red rover. We stood on opposite sides of the house. When the call "Red rover, red rover, let the ball come over!" was made, the team with the ball threw it over the house to the other team. To score a point, the other team had to catch the ball, slip around the house and hit one of the opposing players.

We also played softball, then wandered out to the pasture for a bit of cow chip throwing, seeing who could sail one nearest to the creek.

Mom called when the homemade ice cream was ready. She could tell when it was frozen because the handle on the ice cream freezer would barely turn. Dad always gave it the last few tough cranks.

Mom went out of her way to make my birthdays special. For this party, she frosted the cake, then added a parade of animal crackers around it.

Dad surprised me on each birthday with something I'd been wanting. This year it was a big toy airplane (which I still have). Dad, too, was one of a kind, always smiling and never a stranger to anyone.

Our hometown of Blakely, Georgia, was a Norman Rockwell-type community. Everyone was on a first-name basis, although we kids always addressed adults as "Mister" or "Missus."

After enjoying cake and ice cream at my party, my buddies and I took old pieces of cardboard over to the big sawdust pile not far from our house and took turns sliding down.

Those sweet treats and simple games are permanently etched into my memory.

SIXTH WAS SWEET. Norman Smith (holding the cake) still remembers his sixth birthday party in '42, and he still has the gift from his dad—the toy airplane his friends are holding.

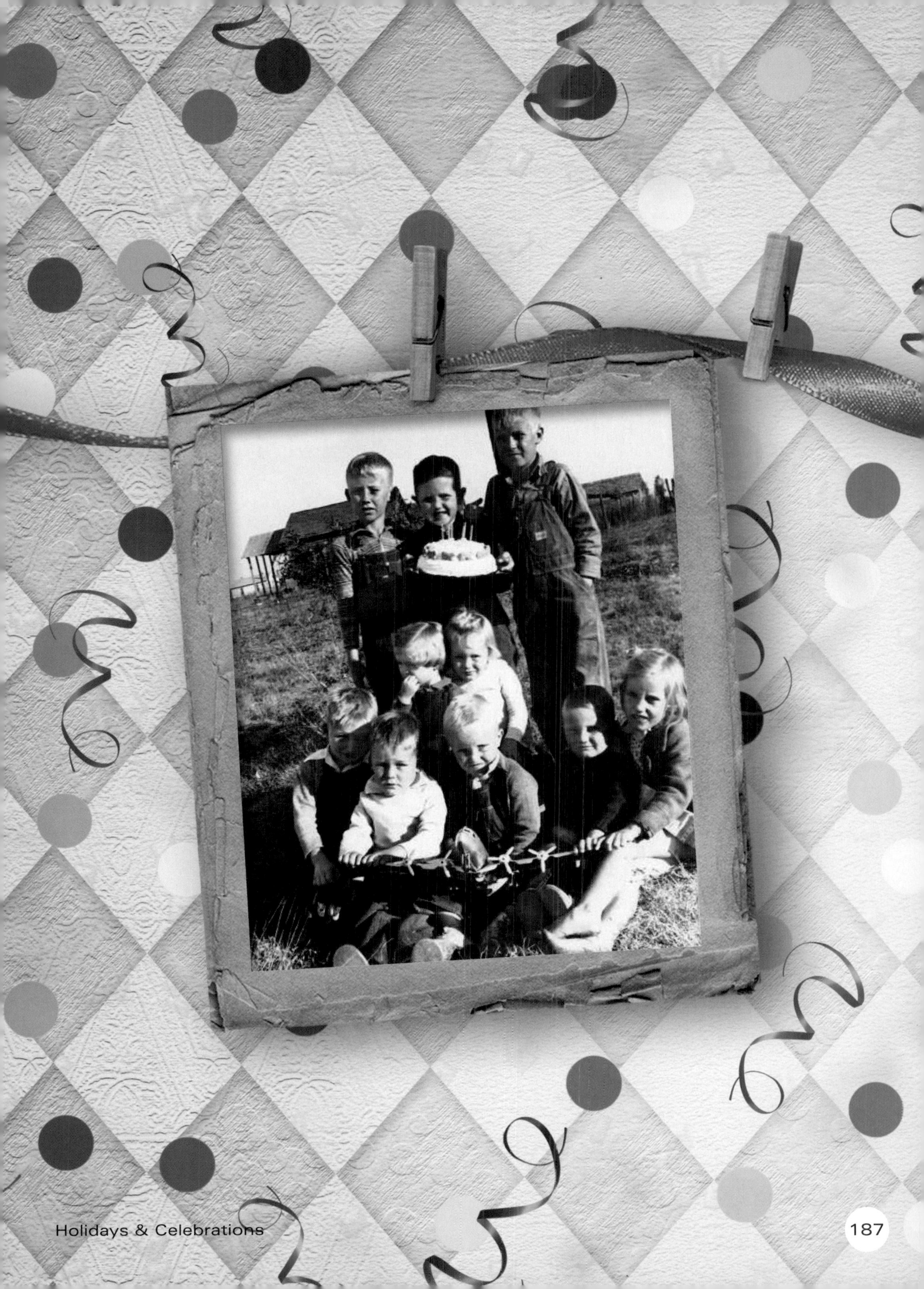

HAVE YOUR CAKE—BUT EAT IT, TOO! "As you can tell by the way she's gazing at it, my daughter, Sheryl, was in complete awe of the doll birthday cake I baked for her seventh birthday, in 1955," says Mrs. Kirk Schwieger of Grand Island, Nebraska. "But she absolutely refused to let me cut it. When Sheryl finally relented a few weeks later, the cake was moldy and inedible!"

ANOTHER YEAR OLDER. Birthdays were momentous occasions. After all, they meant you were inching closer and closer to being a big kid. What would birthday parties be without hats, cake, candles and, most important, the laughter of friends and family?

UNDERWOODARCHIVES.COM

Growing Up

BIRTHDAY SUITED HIM.

"I may have been in the hospital, but my seventh birthday was my best ever," remembers Terrence Dooher of East Syracuse, New York. "A month earlier, in April 1944, I had been hit by a bus while crossing the street, crushing my right leg. On my special day, Mom brought a cake and presents, and we had a little party in my hospital room. Some wounded soldiers joined in the celebration. It wasn't a birthday I would have wished for, but I was happy to be alive!"

DOUBLE THE FUN.

"A 1957 birthday party was held for me and my twin sister Gayle (both wearing orange jumpers), and included another birthday girl, our neighbor Kathy Anders (sitting in front)," notes Linda DeKlein, who is the twin on the left. The other partygoers are (from left) Carol Blok, Laurie VanderKyle and Marilyn Graham. "We were 9, and the party took place in our parents' home near Comstock Park, Michigan," Linda says. "Among the gifts we're holding are a fabric kit to make pot holders and a book about a runaway pancake."

valentine's day delivered fond memories

By Kathleen Jakin, Federal Way, Washington

Thinking of Valentine's Day takes me back to my second-grade class at Holy Redeemer School in Portland, Oregon.

In 1946, our teacher, Sister Ann Mary, converted our simple classroom into a place called Happy Town, complete with street names at the head of each row. In one corner of the room, she assembled a cardboard post office and furnished it with a scale, stamps and a seat for the postmaster. At our desks, each of us made and decorated a mailbox and added our name and address.

For weeks, we would spend our free time drawing, painting and gluing valentines from paper-lace doilies. Sister Ann Mary encouraged us to send a card to everyone in the class. It took a lot of work to write out the envelopes for 40 or so students!

On Valentine's Day, we took our cards to the post office pictured above to get them weighed and stamped. Then several mailmen were selected to deliver our treasures. What suspense! Who would get cards from whom? I don't remember a formal party with treats, but each student intently opened and read each card. At the end of the day, we proudly carried our letters home to share with Mom and Dad.

I'll never forget our dear Sister Ann Mary, who made learning fun!

PASSING LOVE NOTES.
"My old scrapbook is full of old-time valentines (below) from the late 1930s and early 1940s," notes Cloyd Holen of Franklin, Pennsylvania. "What lovely memories from simpler times."

If you don't "COME CLEAN," VALENTINE... I'll just "MOP UP" WITH YOU

TO MY VALENTINE

TO MY VALENTINE

OH YOU "SMOOTHIE" LET'S BE "SUNDAE" DATES!

BLAST FROM THE PAST

One fall day in 1995, my mother, Dorothy Owsley, and I were browsing in an antiques store in our hometown of Owensboro, Kentucky, when I picked up this fancy foldout Valentine's Day card (above).

To my surprise, my mother's maiden name was signed on the back. I asked my mother, "Could this be you?"

She was shocked to see her first-grade teacher's name there as well, handwritten in pencil by my grandfather. It was a valentine that Mother had given her teacher in 1930.

What are the odds that in this city of 54,000, we would find this valentine 65 years later? A card that probably cost less than a dime back then cost us $20 to reclaim, but what a priceless treasure!

—*Barbara Beane, Maceo, Kentucky*

GEE WHIZ! I go for YOU

Like a DUCK goes for water

eggs-cellent easters

COLORED EGGS, CHOCOLATE BUNNIES, EASTER BONNETS— THIS SPRING HOLIDAY WAS BRIMMING WITH TRADITIONS.

STOLEN SWEETS. Suzanne Rydel of Falls Church, Virginia (far right), has a good reason for frowning. She just discovered that her little brother, Danny (next to her), ate all her Easter candy while she was at church!

IN THEIR EASTER BEST. The Clayton family—father Hollis, mother Roberttene, son Thomas Wayne and daughters Peggy Jean (center) and Mary Elaine— are on their way to church on Easter Sunday in 1960. "At the time, Hollis was stationed at Westover Air Force Base in Massachusetts," writes Roberttene, who now lives in Shreveport, Louisiana.

DECORATED EGGS DELIGHTED US. "Every Easter Sunday in the '40s, my family would gather at my mom's parents' home," says Dennis Dye of Wichita, Kansas. "Grandpa would walk the younger children to the chicken house and have us reach under the hens, which would cluck and scare us. Then we'd pull out beautifully colored eggs!"

BYE-BYE, BUNNY. "I always received a chocolate bunny from a family friend for Easter," says Dorothy Everds, Leland, North Carolina (pictured here in 1933). "I'd gaze at it for about 2 weeks before eating it, starting with the ears. I usually made it last for a month after I started nibbling!"

EASTER SMORGASBOARD

Easter Sunday was celebrated at the home of my grandmother. The all-day feast began with a cold breakfast of ham, kielbasa, hard-boiled eggs and a special rye bread from the neighborhood bakery. Mother sculpted a lamb from sticks of butter, with cloves for eyes and a red ribbon around its neck.

The rest of the family came at noon, all the women bearing traditional Polish dishes—pierogies, blintzes, cabbage soup and borscht.

But my most wonderful memories are of the cakes. Each aunt brought her specialty: a pound cake molded into the form of a lamb… poppy seed cake…a special strawberry-banana torte…and a delicious angel food cake with chocolate frosting.

The family has since scattered far and wide, but when I think of those delicious occasions, it's like being there once again.

—*Mike Dahlia, Cedar City, Utah*

When you care enough to send the very best. **Hallmark Cards**

1958

july fourth
festivities

OUR COUNTRY'S BIRTHDAY
WAS CAUSE TO CELEBRATE.

YOUNG OLD GLORIES.
Sisters Betty (on trike) and
Dorothy Small were decorated
with bunting for their annual
Fourth of July parade in 1930.
There was always a parade, says
Betty (now Bearden) of Atlanta,
Georgia, and anybody could join
in. The fire department gave
rides and the fireworks were at
the school stadium.

RIDING HIGH.
Perched atop her pop's
dairy truck in 1923 (she's
on left) Ruth Matheny of
Ormond Beach, Florida,
got a good view of the
July Fourth festivities
in her hometown of
Mankato, Minnesota.

HALLOWEEN

TRICKS AND TREATS MARKED THE OCCASION.

THE GREAT PUMPKIN. Carving jack-o'-lanterns was just the start of the Halloween season. After the pumpkins were scooped clean, Mom would roast pumpkin seeds for us to nibble. Next came a big decision: what to wear for trick-or-treating.

SUPERSTOCK

HE COULDN'T DISGUISE DISAPPOINTMENT

In 1955, when I was in second grade in Storm Lake, Iowa, a note was sent home telling parents about Halloween dress-up day. For some reason, I either lost my note or forgot to give it to my mother.

Imagine my shock when I walked into the classroom on the day of the party to be surrounded by pirates, princesses, ghosts and skeletons. There I was in my usual blue jeans and striped T-shirt.

Each class was to parade through the other rooms to show off their costumes. How embarrassing for me! But my teacher, Mrs. Moulds, saved the day. Instead of having me wait in the classroom, she made me the line leader. I got to hold the pumpkin and lead the parade! Mrs. Moulds made my favorite Halloween the one when I had no costume at all.

—Bari Strader, Forsyth, Missouri

HAPPY HALLOWEEN.

"Every year, Mrs. Katherine Coia hosted a Halloween party for the children in our Hammonton, New Jersey, neighborhood," writes Marion Capelli Condo of Waterford. "Their home was in a beautiful rural area with lots of farms. At the party we played games, bobbed for apples and ate delicious treats. I'm the little cowgirl seated in the middle. I didn't want my picture taken because I had fallen and had a bruise on my chin."

FRIGHT NIGHT.

Remember those plastic Halloween masks that made your face all sweaty? This slide from Halloween night 1967 was shared by Brenda Ross of Fayetteville, North Carolina. Her daughter Denise (left), 4, was trick-or-treating with cousins Matt, 4, and Jimmy, 2, in Wallingford, Connecticut.

RDA-GID

food and family were the focus of thanksgiving

By the time the 22-pound turkey shown at right was done roasting at my grandmother's house, all of us eager grandchildren had done our part to help fix the feast. (I'm the hungry lad in back, third from left.) My dad, Vin, captured our family's typical Thanksgiving in this 1963 photo.

We grandchildren had the "privilege" of polishing the pans, mashing the turnips and potatoes, and making sugar cookies out of the extra homemade piecrust. I assure you Grandma's pie was made with rhubarb from her garden and had the flakiest crust. She would never use a boxed crust mix or canned fruit. Grandma always lamented, "You just can't get a good loaf of bread today."

Hours before this photo was taken, it's safe to say we were all glued to the TV set to watch the Macy's Thanksgiving Day Parade.

After dinner, everyone would pile into their family's station wagon and drive to downtown Bridgeport for the traditional first lighting of the Christmas lights.

—*Mike Simko, Bridgeport, Connecticut*

double yum!

"In 1958, Thanksgiving was an especially happy day for the Stevens family living at Whiteman Air Force Base, Missouri," relates M.R. Stevens of Huntsville, Alabama. "It also happens that Annemarie, 3, got her Thanksgiving turkey leg and a baby sister on the same day!"

1946

christmases to remember

SCARED BY SANTA

Every Christmas Eve, my one wish was to see Santa Claus deliver the gifts to our house. I always had a plan to catch him in the act, but none ever worked.

In 1944, my plan was foiled yet again. After I'd opened my presents, I decided to visit my best friend, who lived in an apartment down the street, to see what Santa had brought him. When I arrived, his family was still waiting for the man in the red suit, so after a brief visit I said goodbye. As I carefully made my way down the dim, creepy stairway to the outside door, it opened—and in walked Santa! I was caught completely off guard. Petrified, I ran home as fast as my feet would carry me.

I didn't tell a soul about my Christmas Eve adventure—not even my best friend. In the years to follow, I never again planned to watch for Santa. We'd already met!

—Bob Staab, Two Rivers, Wisconsin

WHITE CHRISTMAS WISHES. "When my brother, Michael, and I visited Santa in 1950, my mom says I asked him for snow," says Leslee Decaire of North Olmsted, Ohio. "Since we were living in Florida at the time, that was too tall an order for him to fill!"

YULETIDE PERFORMANCE.

"This 1948 picture shows me (in striped outfit) and other neighborhood kids putting on our annual Christmas pageant for our parents," says Roberta Reid of Mansfield, Ohio. "Back then, we didn't get a lot of gifts and our decorations were usually homemade, but Christmas was always merry for us!"

DAD'S PRESENCE WAS BEST.

"My brother, George, and sister, Betty Jean, weren't bothered that the Aeroflite wagon and baby doll were the only presents they received the Christmas of 1946," writes Dolores Robertson, Adah, Pennsylvania. "They were just happy that Dad had returned from the Army the month before so we could celebrate the holiday as a family once again."

SANTA FILLED STOCKINGS WITH FAMILY'S HELP

It was a somewhat slim Christmas for us five Weber sisters (from left, Patsy, Janet, me, Joyce and Carole) while living in Ponca City, Oklahoma, in 1949.

The new bathrobes and slippers Santa left us were actually made by our mother. She'd used pink and blue flannel our grandmother bought for the project.

Our uncle Elmo made the stockings from bright red oilcloth. Uncle Elmo was a career Marine, and we seldom saw him. It's a wonder he didn't misspell more names than just Carole's! But he helped out Santa by filling the stockings with coloring books and small toys.

Our only other gift from Santa was a metal dollhouse. My mother's cousin had five boys who came over one day. We never forgave them for sitting on the dollhouse and wrecking it!

—*Marilee Weber Camblin*
Portland, Oregon

MISSED SANTA BY SECONDS. "One Christmas Eve some 40 years ago, my sister and I were taking a bath when we heard sleigh bells ring and Dad exclaim, 'Hello, Santa!'" remembers Paula Hlucky, Parma Heights, Ohio. "Debbie and I were frightened yet excited. Mom couldn't wash us, dress us and set our hair in curlers fast enough.

"We ran from the bathroom and down the hall only to hear the sleigh bells ring again. When Debbie and I reached the living room, Santa was gone! But the room was aglow and presents were under the tree. Now every time I hear sleigh bells, I fondly recall how Debbie (on right in photo) and I almost got to see Santa making Christmas merry."

FAKE-OUT. Artie Maglionico's cousins (from left) John, Lou Ann and Maria had one of the first artificial Christmas trees in Lodi, New Jersey.

THE GREAT UNVEILING. After the kids went to bed on Christmas Eve, my parents would decorate the tree in the front room. The next morning, after Mom got us ready, she'd line up all 11 of us in the dining room and we'd cover someone else's eyes with our hands. Then she would lead us into the front room to see the tree. My heart always beat so fast, and I bet the others' did, too. We knew that when she told us to put down our hands, we'd be standing in front of the most beautiful tree in the world, like this one from 1948!

—Bonnie Hansen, Omaha, Nebraska

O, CHRISTMAS TREES

People in my extended family seem to have a soft spot for Christmas trees with particularly sparse branches. Each year, without fail, the tree my family took home was always the most undernourished one on the lot—and it looked even worse after my dad hacked away at it until it fit in the stand.

But my mother had a knack for making even the skimpiest tree pass for a display at Rockefeller Center. Once we turned on the multicolored lights, I knew Christmas had officially arrived.

The artificial tree at my cousins' house sparks a similar memory. It was so short on branches that when the blue lights went on, it looked like a chest x-ray. When my cousins started growing taller than the tree, my uncle gave it a place of honor on a decorated card table.

—Artie Maglionico, Lodi, New Jersey

MAGICAL MEMORIES. "In our family, we opened presents on Christmas Eve," recalls Lois Hasenfratz of Florissant, Missouri. "After supper, my sister, Marilyn, and I were told to go to the basement and wait. When we were safely out of sight, the doorbell would ring and heavy footsteps would sound on the floor above us. Hearing Mom say goodbye to Santa was the signal to race back upstairs to see what he'd left.

"My aunt snapped this photo of me and Marilyn in 1956. I remember we tried to sit as close to the tree as possible in an effort to sneak a look at how many presents we'd gotten."

> *There's nothing sadder in this world than to awake Christmas morning and not be a child.*
> —ERMA BOMBECK

SEALED WITH A WISH. "Remember when letters to Santa Claus were deposited in a little house like this in front of City Hall?" writes Margaret Rostedt of Montebello, California. "This photo was taken in White Plains, New York, in 1930 or '31. That's me mailing the letter as my brother and a friend attempt to peek into the house. My coat was sewn from my mom's old one—the material was turned inside out."

confettied kids

"On New Year's Day 1961, two of our children, Stanley (left) and Sally, offered to help clean up the living room after a New Year's Eve party," relates Harry Sheppard from San Mateo, California. 'The kids decided to have their own New Year's party by draping themselves with confetti."

My Childhood Memories

My Childhood Memories